WESTBURY CEMENT WORKS
AN ILLUSTRATED HISTORY

Simon Knight

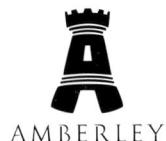

AMBERLEY

First published 2018

Amberley Publishing
The Hill, Stroud
Gloucestershire, GL5 4EP

www.amberley-books.com

Copyright © Simon Knight, 2018

The right of Simon Knight to be identified as the Author
of this work has been asserted in accordance with the
Copyrights, Designs and Patents Act 1988.

All rights reserved. No part of this book may be reprinted
or reproduced or utilised in any form or by any electronic,
mechanical or other means, now known or hereafter invented, including photocopying and recording,
or in any information
storage or retrieval system, without the permission in writing
from the Publishers.

British Library Cataloguing in Publication Data.
A catalogue record for this book is available from the British Library.

ISBN 978 1 4456 7392 9 (print)
ISBN 978 1 4456 7393 6 (ebook)

Typesetting and Origination by Amberley Publishing.
Printed in Great Britain.

Contents

	Introduction	4
Chapter 1	A Valued Place of Work	6
Chapter 2	The Emergence of a New Industry	7
Chapter 3	What is Cement?	10
Chapter 4	The Raw Materials Required in the Production of Cement – Chalk and Clay	12
Chapter 5	Kiln and Chimney Construction	23
Chapter 6	A Ghost Town	44
Chapter 7	Hidden Wildlife	49
Chapter 8	Deadly Doris	67
Chapter 9	Chimney Demolition	72
Chapter 10	The End of Cement Production at Westbury	94
	Acknowledgements	96

Introduction

My introduction to Westbury Cement Works took place on 26 February 2016. It was a Saturday, and the recently started demolition of the site had stopped for the weekend. The day was cold and dull, and I will be honest, after that first visit I didn't want to ever go back.

Two friends, Andy and Rob, had suggested that we try to get permission to go in and get some aerial video and stills of the site before it got demolished, as it would be good material to have to help showcase my newly formed aerial photography business, Skynamite. Somewhat reluctantly, I went along with the idea. After getting permission from Tarmac (who own the cement works), on a cold and dull February morning we

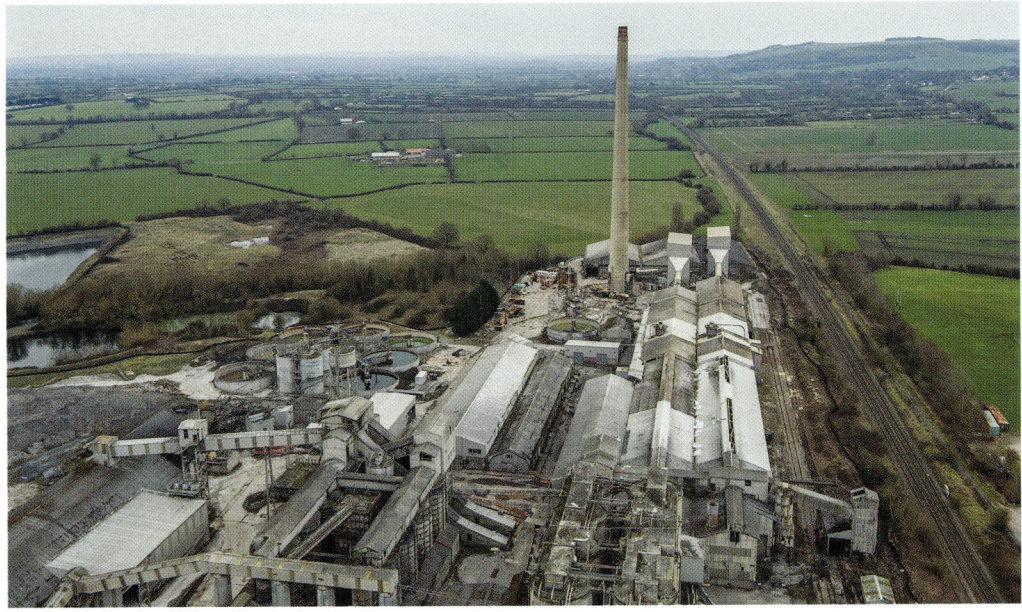

The first day on site, 27 February 2016. The demolition had barely started, and the excavators are lying dormant at the east end of the site (close to the chimney). The long buildings on the right, next to the rail siding, are the kiln houses. Both electrostatic precipitators are still connected to their respective kilns but have been disconnected from the base of the chimney.

Introduction

donned our PPE gear and met Nigel Osman, who at this time was the Estate Warden. He gave us a safety briefing and would keep an eye on us, make sure we were safe and advise us of where we could operate from.

I could find no enthusiasm for what I was doing there. The entire colour palette of the site was an uninspiring grey, and almost everything seemed to be covered in dust. To add to my feelings of gloom, there were frustrating problems with the drones – it was difficult to find somewhere to take off from without getting compass or GPS errors. At times, I could barely feel my thumbs while flying due to the lack of temperature. It was a bit of a nightmare to say the least! The only positives that I could take away from that first visit was that it was mighty impressive to be stood so close to the 400-foot-tall chimney that I had only ever seen from afar, and I did get to see the site's pair of peregrine falcons. I love wildlife, so this really was a highlight for me. I left the site that day thinking that I would never go back again.

But go back I did. A few days later Nigel gave myself and Andy a tour of the site before the demolition crew started work that day. We walked the length of the two huge rotary kilns while Nigel told stories about working life on site and what happened at this once busy place. Slowly, the works started to have more meaning to me. It was no longer this ghostly, dusty, empty shell of a place; it was somewhere that was once alive, somewhere that once thrived and provided jobs. It had given security to families and it had provided the cement that held together buildings all over the country. Maybe even your house is held together by cement that was produced at Westbury Cement Works. I began to realise how important a place it had been.

On that day, I distinctly remember standing at the base of the chimney and feeling dizzy, and just a little bit intimidated as I looked up in awe to its brick top, towering 400 feet above me. I had no idea that seven months later I would be back here at 4 a.m., preparing to film this iconic Wiltshire landmark being brought to the ground.

Over the next few months the site would slowly endear itself to me as I learned of its past, as I met its employees, and as I watched the huge machinery and buildings that once helped to power a thriving industry being pulled to the ground and taken off site as scrap metal in 30-ton lorry loads.

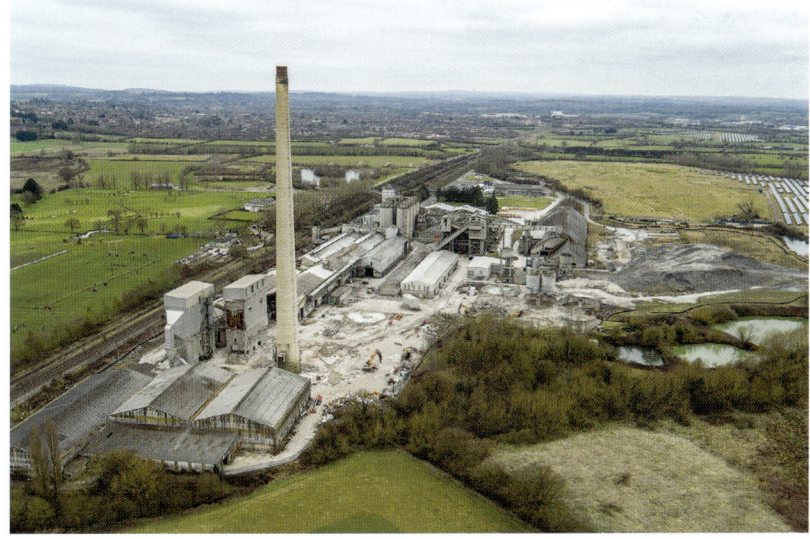

Looking west towards Westbury. Now the kiln feed mixer, compressor building and dust wetting silo have been removed. Demolition has also started on the slurry mixers. 20 March 2016.

Chapter 1

A Valued Place of Work

What does it mean to work somewhere? It means you can pay your bills, it means you can support your family, it means you have somewhere to go from 9 a.m. to 5.30 p.m. It means security. But what do you get from working somewhere? What you get from working somewhere is ultimately what you put into it. You can put only the minimum into your work and simply take home your pay cheque and forget about it. If that's what makes you happy, then fine. But you can choose to put your heart into your work and you can take home more than your pay cheque. You can take home lasting friendships, you can take home a feeling of satisfaction, accomplishment and contribution. Your work becomes something that has purpose, that has meaning and becomes a place where you belong. This is what the cement works meant to many of its employees.

I have met a cement works employee who couldn't bring himself to watch the demolition of the works' iconic chimney in person, and then later was almost moved to tears while watching our drone footage of the chimney falling earlier that day.

Seeing what the cement works meant to that employee is what gave me that 'light bulb' moment – it made me realise that soon the bulk of what went on there would be nothing more than a distant memory and that maybe it would be a good idea to do something to help preserve that memory.

Throughout these pages my hope is that I can respectfully reflect that passion I saw in one man's eyes and that I can leave this book as something that people will look at not with mournful eyes, but with fond memories of a place that meant something to them and to the community. I also hope that people with no connection to Westbury Cement Works may find the book interesting as the place was more than a tall chimney that could be seen from miles around. Rather, it was a place that had its own unique character; it provided for the community; it was part of a vital and once thriving industry; it was conscious of the environment; and it helped reveal an ancient history that would have likely remained hidden without the construction of the works taking place.

Chapter 2

The Emergence of a New Industry

During the dawn of the UK cement industry there was an abundance of small companies in operation. However, during the last decade of the nineteenth century, overseas competition grew and more cement was being imported into Britain. This lead to a flurry of mergers within the British industry and in 1900 the Associated Portland Cement Manufacturers Ltd (APCM) was formed out of an amalgamation of twenty-four small, struggling cement producers. But there would be difficult times ahead and it wasn't until the construction industry recovered after the First World War and the Great Depression that cement production began to increase again.

In 1945, the first meeting was held with the War Office (which was one of the five Departments of State that would later merge to form the Ministry of Defence) over the purchase of the land that lay on the edge of the military firing ranges on Salisbury Plain and overlooked the town of Westbury, in Wiltshire. This land formed part of the escarpment that is home to the well-known White Horse. Records suggest that the horse was originally cut into the hillside in the late 1600s and that this was likely done to commemorate the Battle of Ethandun, which was thought to have taken place at Bratton Camp in AD 878. This land would be where the all-important chalk quarry would be located. Locating the chalk quarry on top of the escarpment, south-west of the White Horse, would be the perfect location as it meant that the quarry works could be concealed deep down below the escarpment and would only be visible when standing on the edge of the quarry itself.

Initially, the military were opposed to the sale of the land because of the possibility of interference with the firing ranges. At the request of Blue Circle Industries Ltd, the Ministry of Town and Country Planning applied pressure to the War Department and in the summer of 1946 the sale was agreed. The initial asking price for the land was £400 per acre, but it is believed that the War Department had originally acquired the land for about £18 per acre during the First World War.

The Minister of Town and Country Planning decided that a public inquiry should be held, looking into the company's application for planning permission for the chalk quarry and for the building of the works. Subsequently, further negotiations on the purchase were deferred until the Minister's decision in principle became known in the summer of 1947. There then followed a period of sporadic negotiations against the background of the expropriations of development rights under the 1947 Planning Act. With regards to the question of price, the Minister of Town and Country Planning was again requested to step in. He advised that the company could expect a more favourable approach. The final agreement was reached, and in September 1948 a price of £29 per acre was agreed. With the chalk quarry land secured, the company now needed to secure land for the works site and the clay quarry.

The site where the works was to be had belonged to the Westbury Iron Company, which had gone into voluntary liquidation. It was put to the bank that had ownership of the site that they could expect no more for the land than had been paid to the War Department. Therefore, the £29 per acre also stood for the works site and its clay reserves. This meant that the overall cost of the acquisition of the land for the chalk and clay quarries and the works site was under £10,000. To this day, this likely remains one of the cheapest industrial developments (from a land point of view) in the entire country. This was partly due to a delay of thirteen years between acquiring planning permission and the actual construction of the works.

As soon as planning permission had been received, the company built the road access into the works and excavated the area that was required for the rail sidings. By doing this, if planning permission had later been revoked, it meant that the company was liable for compensation, as expenditure had been incurred. The site then lay dormant, as no further development took place for thirteen years. During this period of dormancy, development charges under the 1947 Act were abolished, so the original land purchase price of £29 remained. Also, the threat of the cement industry becoming nationalised had gone, and with large-scale projects such as motorway building on the increase, the demand for cement had increased dramatically.

Due to strong opposition against the development of the site, Lewis Silkin, the Minister of Housing and Local Government, intervened. The opposition claimed that Blue Circle had always had ambitions for a works of much larger capacity, despite the fact that it had only asked for a works with a capacity of 150,000 tons. The claim was that the company was simply trying to get the permission through, and once sited there would seek to increase capacity. There was also a water problem. Boreholes in the area were very shallow and the public feared that with its own additional borehole the works' water requirements would have a negative effect on the capacity of existing wells. To overcome these issues, Mr Silkin did not restrict the productive capacity of the works. Instead, he imposed a condition in the planning permission that the water usage would not exceed 77,000 gallons per day, which was sufficient for a cement production of 150,000 tons per year. Given that the company did aspire to an annual cement production capacity higher than initially asked for, this was a problem. However, it was solved by doing a deal with the Urban District Council, which meant that the works would use water that came directly from the local sewage treatment plant. This water would have otherwise gone into a tributary of the River Avon, so the solution not only enabled the water demands of an increased capacity to be met, it also had a positive effect on the environment.

The works started cement production as a single kiln operation in 1962, and on 29 April 1963 Sir Robert Grimston, Bt., MP for Westbury, formally declared the works open with a wish that the industry might prosper to the advantage of all those engaged in it. During the ceremony many guests were in attendance, including government officials, architects, engineers, local contractors and representatives of the building industry, who were welcomed by Mr J. A. E. Reiss, Mr V. C. Ellison and Mr A. Poole. In his introduction, Mr Reiss said that the Westbury Cement Works would have a life of at least sixty years, which meant the production of around 18 million tons of cement. This lifespan would see the works provide enough concrete to construct 4 million homes or 10,000 miles of six-lane concrete motorway. He said that the opening of the works tied up with the programme of rail-supplied bulk-cement plants in the West Country that were now completed. He went on to thank the people of Westbury and all those in the Planning Authorities who had made the opening of the works possible. He spoke about Sir Robert Grimston and Mr R. C. Grenfell, whose support had been invaluable since the first public inquiry back in 1947.

Mr Reiss said that everything possible had been done to make the plant an attractive works and he hoped that in the course of time it would be considered as blending in as well as possible with its beautiful surroundings. He hoped that for many years the works would bring employment to the people of Westbury, their sons, and their grandsons.

Sir Robert Grimston said that it was with great pleasure that he had accepted the invitation to perform the opening ceremony and that the works was of national interest and the interest to the whole of Westbury, going on to add: 'To quote a cliché, the production of cement in ever increasing quantities is required all of the time.' Westbury had all of the natural ingredients for efficient cement production – chalk, clay, water and transport facilities. He also felt that the works would help to reduce the amount of industry that was heavily concentrated around London.

He was pleased that, once the ministerial decision had been made to go ahead with the works, the company received nothing but co-operation from the local authorities. Sir Robert congratulated the company and all who took part in the building of the works. This included local firms, without whose support it would not have been successful. He also thanked the company for doing as much as possible to preserve the amenities. He added that he had recently been up to the White Horse and felt that the works with its white plume might even add to the landscape!

Chapter 3

What is Cement?

Cement is something that most of us take for granted, or simply don't even think about. Yet it is something that we all depend upon. It helps provide us with shelter in the construction of our homes and places of work, and it helps us get to work and on holiday with the construction of our roads and runways. Quite simply, society would not be where it is today without the discovery of cement.

At the simplest level, cement derives from heating together a mixture of finely ground limestone and clay to create a powder that hardens with the addition of water. The use of cement as a building material dates back thousands of years: the Egyptians mixed

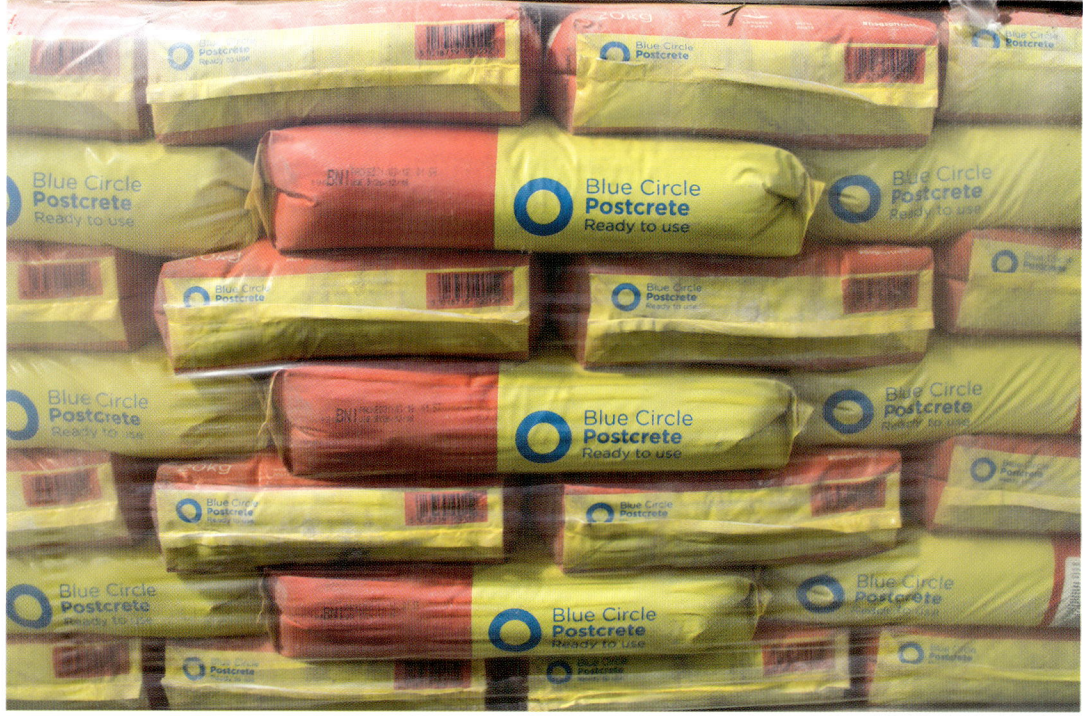

Postcrete, a high-value product for Tarmac.

burnt lime with gypsum as a cement and the Romans added crushed volcanic ash to lime to form a cement. The Romans found that this cement would set underwater and it was used for the construction of harbours.

The big breakthrough came with the discovery of Portland cement. Joseph Aspdin, who was a bricklayer in Leeds, took out a patent for his 'Portland' cement in 1824. He produced this cement by firing finely ground clay and limestone until the limestone was calcined. Calcination occurs in kilns under high temperatures and is the decomposition of calcium carbonate (limestone) to calcium oxide (lime). Aspdin named his cement 'Portland', because its colour resembled that of Portland stone, which occurs naturally in Southern England.

In 1845, Isaac Johnson made the first modern Portland cement. He mixed chalk and clay in proportion with water at much higher temperatures of 1,400–1,500 °C, where clinkering occurs. Clinker is the relatively small (up to 25 millimetres) lumps that form by the fusing together without melting of the chalk and clay. It is this Portland cement, using chalk and clay slurry, that was the most familiar cement that Westbury Cement Works produced from 1962, through to 2009. The works also produced a specialised masonry cement called Walcrete, a rapid hardening cement called Ferrocrete, and Mastercrete, which is essentially a Portland cement but with improved properties that is used in concrete, mortar, rendering and screeds. Mastercrete later superseded Walcrete.

Chapter 4

The Raw Materials Required in the Production of Cement – Chalk and Clay

The Chalk Quarry

The chalk that is quarried from the escarpment to the south-west of the White Horse was extracted down to the grey chalk, approximately 65 meters below the surface, using large excavators and dump trucks. The dump trucks transferred the chalk to a crusher, where it was reduced to lumps approximately 9 inches in size. The chalk was then fed into the wash mill, where it was smashed and crushed with water to form the chalk slurry. It emerged from grids in the sides of the wash mill when the correct particle size had been reached. The rough slurry would then pass into the screening mill. This operated in the same way

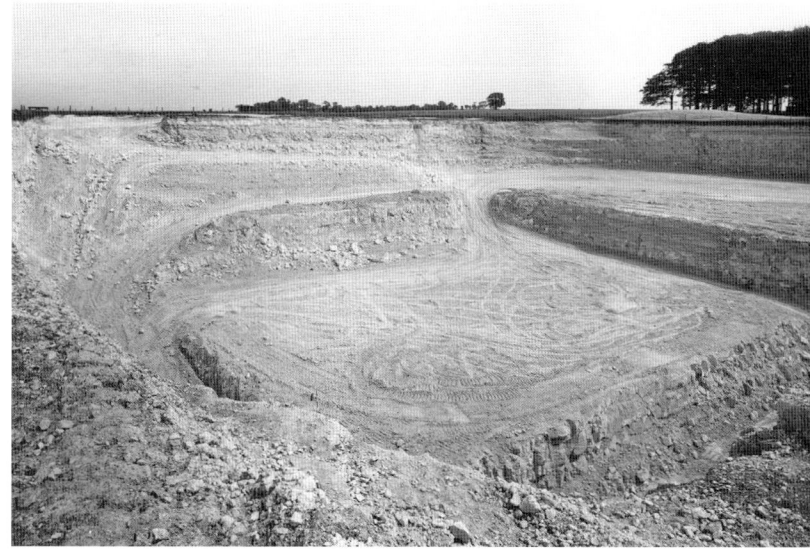

The chalk quarry, ready for work to start on the construction of the mills. 20 July 1961.

as the wash mill, only the grids in the side of the mill were much finer, thus producing a finer slurry. After the screening mill, the slurry passed into a sump, where it was pumped through sieve bends to a finished slurry tank. Any oversized material from the sieve bends was returned to a regrind mill for further grinding. The last stage in processing the chalk was for the slurry to be pumped to a storage mixer at the top of the escarpment, from where it would be gravity-fed underground, almost a mile and quarter down to the works.

When cement demand was at its highest, over a million tons of chalk was moved from the quarry to the works each year, and because the quarry was concealed within the White Horse escarpment and the chalk was fed through an underground pipeline to the works, the whole process had no negative impact on the aesthetics of the environment.

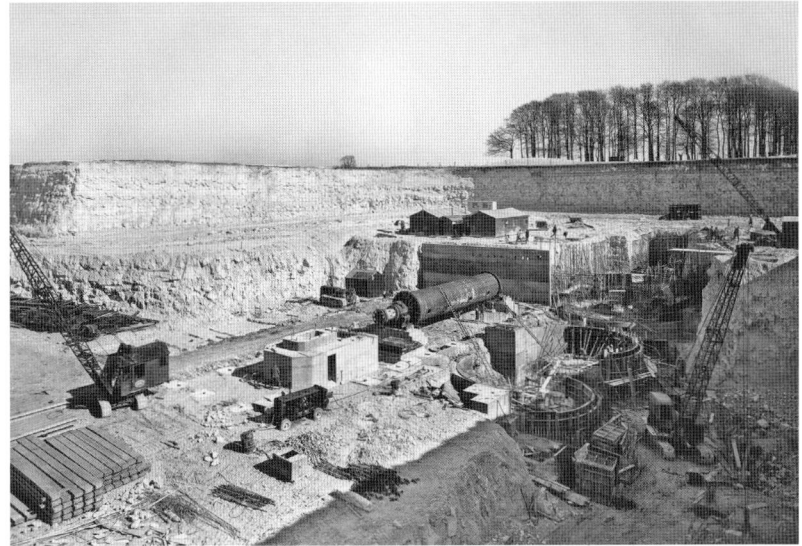

The primary mills are now being installed. 8 March 1962.

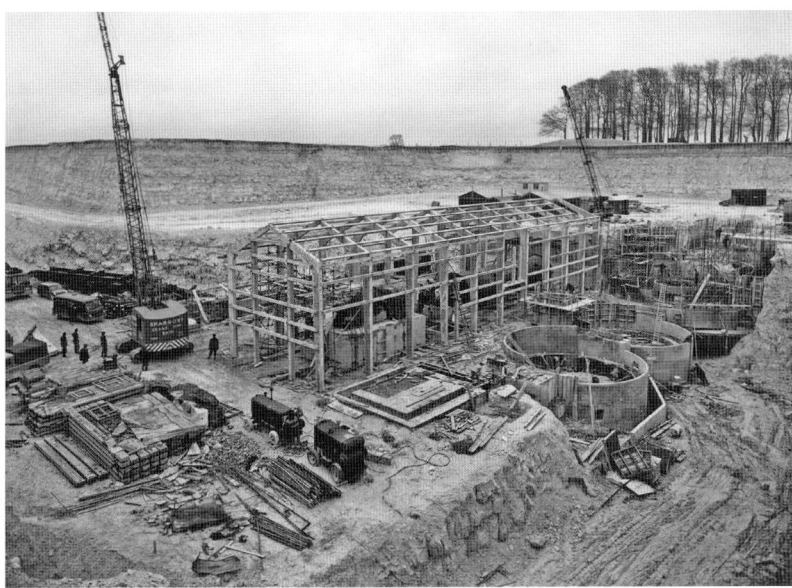

The mill building framework is now in place as construction of the screening mill progresses. 11 April 1962.

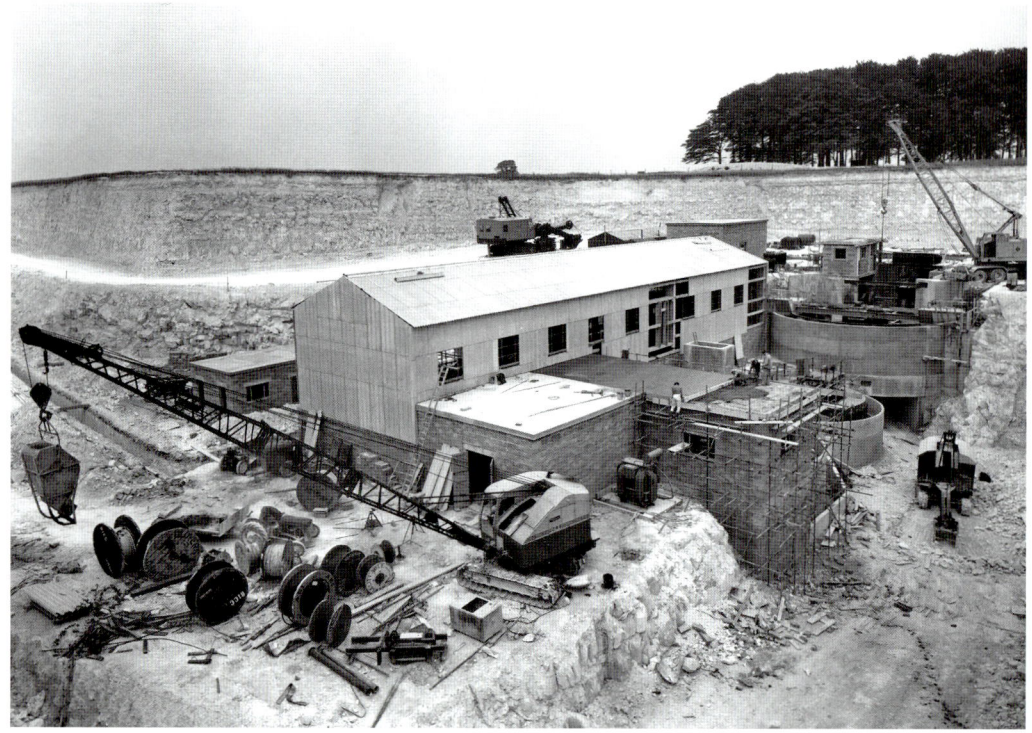

The mill building, now clad in asbestos-cement sheeting. 8 July 1962.

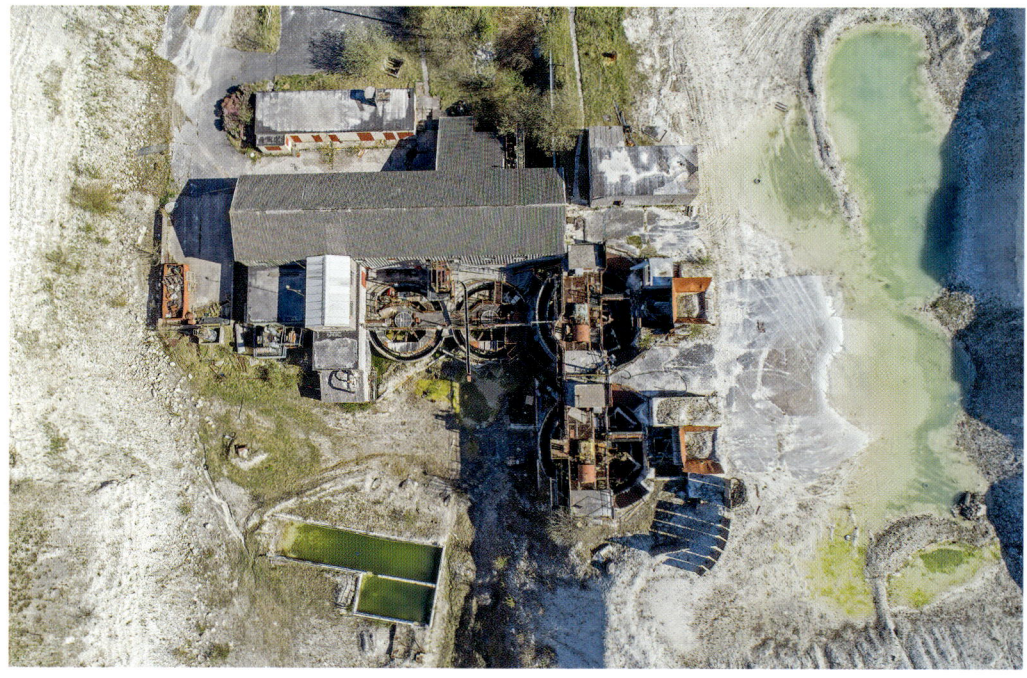

The mothballed quarry mills seen in 2018.

The Raw Materials Required in the Production of Cement

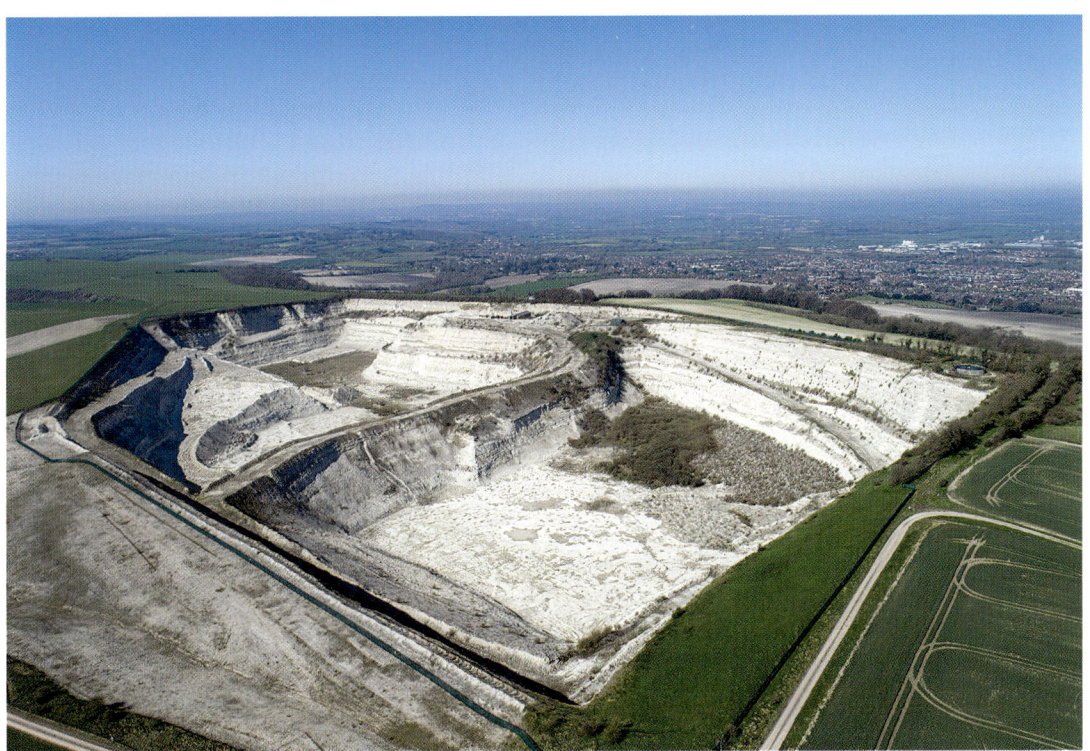

The chalk quarry as it is now. It is approximately 870 metres across its longest side (left to right in the picture) and has a perimeter of approximately 2,560 metres. The deepest part of the quarry is approximately 65 metres below surface level. Its true size can only be appreciated from the air. Westbury lies below, to the north-west, and some of its residents probably don't even realise the quarry is there.

The Clay Quarry

The clay quarry, now filled with water, is situated in the north-west corner of the works. This particular clay is known as Kimmeridge Clay and is of significant geological importance, as will be discussed later.

The process of washing the clay is very similar to that of the chalk, using one rough mill and two screening mills. An extra addition to the process at Westbury was a slurry mixture of sand and iron oxide via a tube mill. The mixing together of the chalk, clay, sand and iron oxide in controlled proportions resulted in the final recipe from which the cement clinker was manufactured. The correct preparation of these raw materials is extremely important. Works laboratories took slurry samples to monitor and ensure that the correct percentages of the required materials were present. This was done using an X-ray frequency analyser to ensure ideal quality. The final slurry was stored in storage mixers before being pumped into the back end of the kilns. Almost all of the water used in the slurry making process was recycled from the local sewage works, as mentioned, and this was another way the works demonstrated its conscientious approach to the environment.

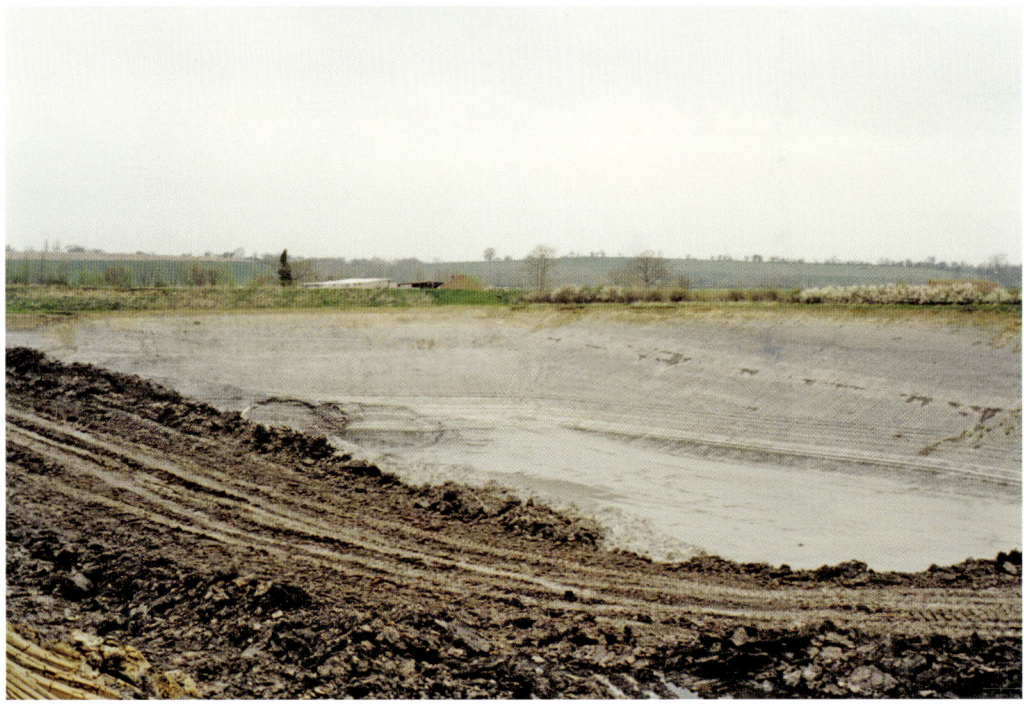

The early diggings of the clay quarry. The date that this picture was taken is not known, but it would have been after 1994.

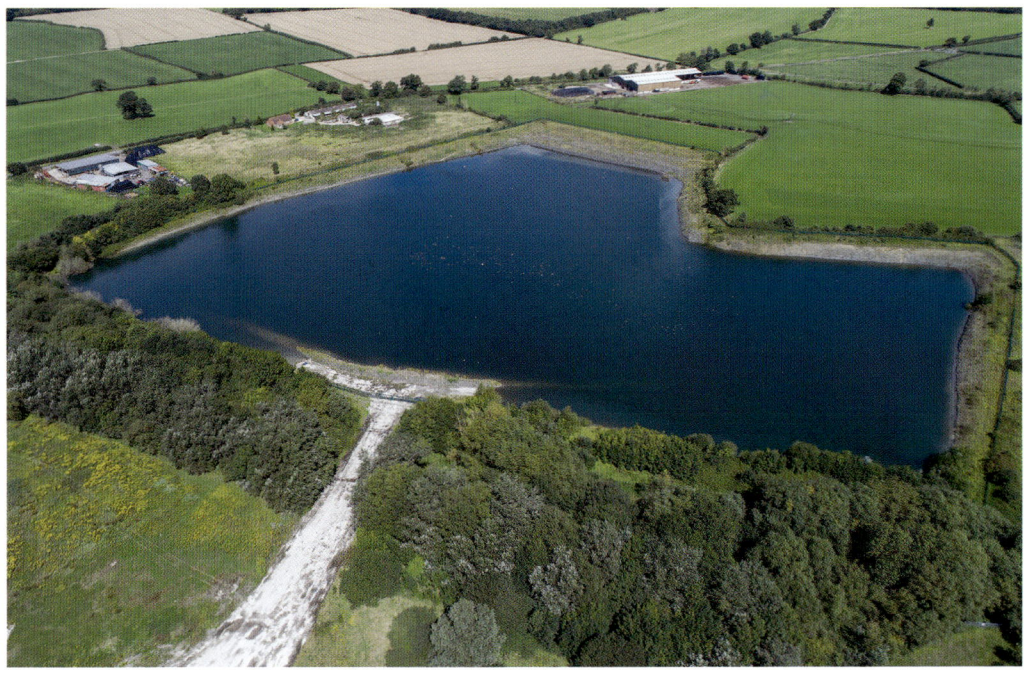

The clay quarry now, home to waterfowl and hiding ancient secrets.

The Raw Materials Required in the Production of Cement

The Rotary Kilns

At the heart of the cement making process at the works were its two huge rotary kilns. Made by the steelmakers and ship builders Vickers-Armstrong, each steel kiln was 4.2 meters in diameter and inclined at an angle of approximately 2 degrees. Kiln No. 1 measured 450 feet and Kiln No. 2 was slightly longer at 500 feet. Each of the kilns were lined with thousands of firebricks, which were vital in helping to contain the high temperatures of up to 1,400 °C that were generated towards the front (lowest and hottest) end of each kiln as they rotated clockwise (when viewed from the front end) at around 1.2 revolutions per minute.

Each kiln was capable of producing around 1,000 tons of cement clinker per day. The process started with slurry, whose moisture was around 36 per cent, being introduced into the back end of the kiln, travelling downhill towards the front end of the kiln as it rotated. A series of chains that hung in the first 30 per cent (from the back end) of the kiln provided a means of heat transfer to the newly introduced slurry. In the first main zone of the kiln – the drying zone – water was driven off from the slurry at temperatures between 150 and 200 degrees centigrade. In the second zone – the calcining, or decarbonating zone – the chalk separated from the calcium carbonate to give carbon dioxide and lime. This took place at temperatures of up to 1,000 °C. The final zone of the kiln was the burning zone. Here, at temperatures up to 1,400 °C, the hot lime reacted with the silica and the alumina from the clay to form complex aluminates and silicates. The great strength of cement is derived from the formation of these compounds.

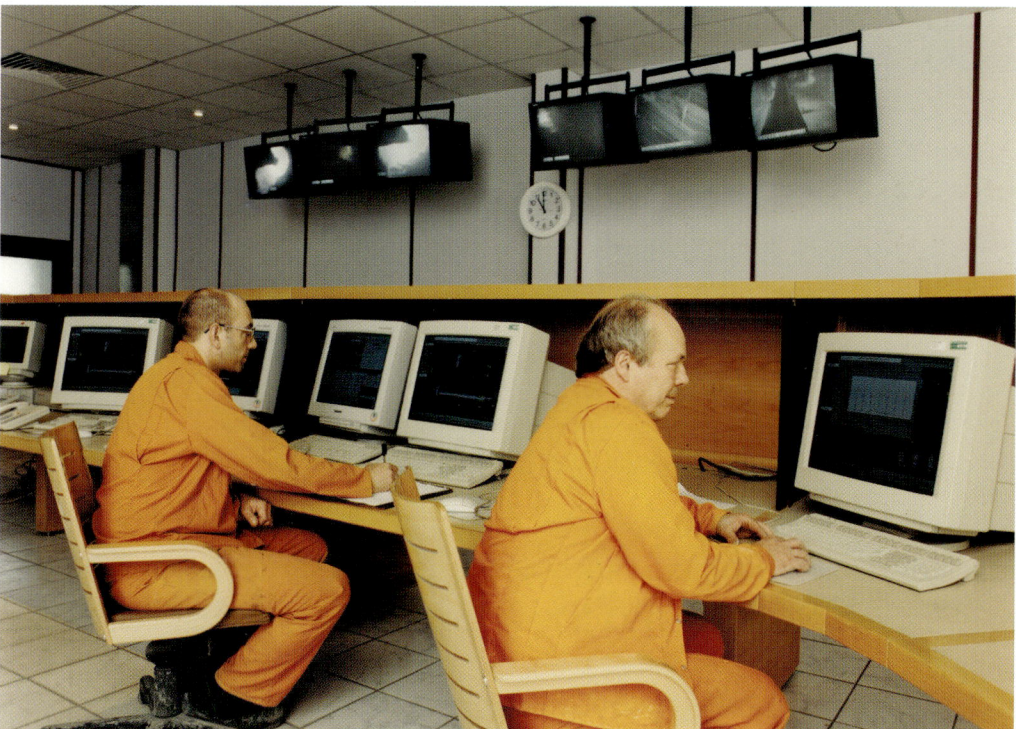

Here, the employee on the left is monitoring the kilns. The two outside screens on the left are displaying images relayed back from Spyrometer cameras and are looking into the hot end of the kiln.

The kilns used a fully automated control system and, when the technology was available, had a computer back up that allowed them to be run on 'autopilot' for long periods of time.

The high temperatures in the kiln were achieved by pulverised coal being blown in through the burner pipe, which produced a large concentric flame in the front end of the kiln. To fuel the burner, around 3,000 tons per week of pulverised coal fuel were delivered by rail from an open-cast mine in South Wales.

The works greatest overhead was its energy bill, which prompted a drive to burn domestic refuse as a supplement to the coal. From the late 1970s through to the early 1980s, the works used approximately 60,000 tons of pulverised refuse in the kilns. In another drive to supplement the coal fuel and to further reduce costs, in the 1990s Westbury became the first Blue Circle works to burn used vehicle tyres. During this period Bridgestone used the works to dispose of their used Formula 1 tyres. At the time, Bridgestone were involved in a tyre war with Michelin and they were also making bespoke tyres, custom made for Michael Schumacher, so they were keen to avoid their tyres getting into the wrong hands. To that end, Bridgestone would deliver the tyres directly to the kiln and oversee the loading of the tyres to the feed, wanting the secrets of their compounds to be thoroughly incinerated. However, they didn't hang around to see the tyres fall into the kiln, where there were works employees waiting! Bridgestone only used the works to dispose of their tyres a couple of times, as their tyres caused problems. Being a performance tyre, their construction was very lightweight and flimsy once removed from the wheel. This caused them to sometimes get stuck on the

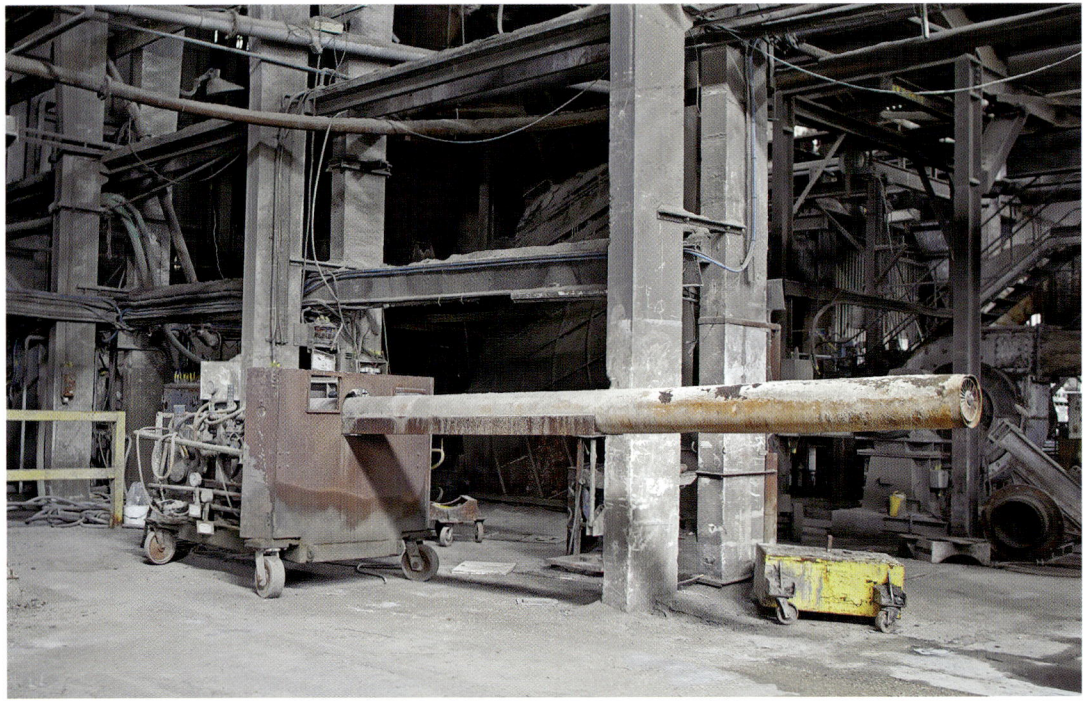

The burner that provides the flame to the hot end of the kiln. This would be saved from the demolition and is still on site today.

The Raw Materials Required in the Production of Cement

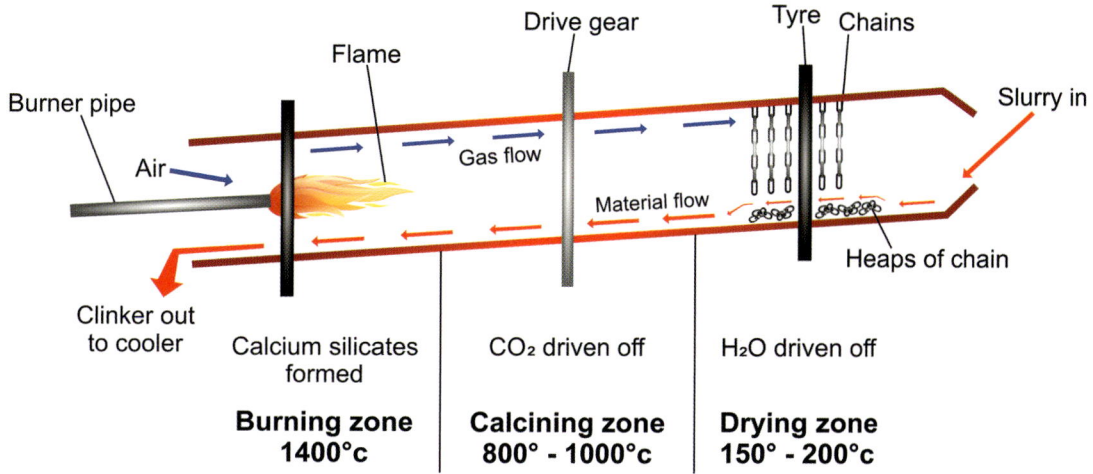

A diagram of the kiln. (Courtesy Louis Smith)

feed, resulting in an employee having to manually move the tyre along. When the feed of tyres was interrupted, this caused heat issues within the kiln and the works couldn't afford the down time of having to manually handle the tyres, so the Formula 1 tyre deliveries were short lived.

As the clinker travelled down the kiln, it reached its peak temperature as it passed under the flame, before it dropped out of the kiln into the cooler. Air was first drawn through the cooler and then through the kiln to aid with the combustion of the coal. The air in the cooler was heated by the cooling clinker and would reach temperatures of 400 to 800 °C, which caused intense and rapid combustion of the coal.

The cement clinker emerged from the kiln at approximately 1,000 °C. It fell down onto a moving grate cooler, through which cold air was blown from a series of fans that were situated underneath the grate. The clinker left the cooler at a temperature of approximately 80 °C, at which point it would pass via a bucket conveyor to eight 1,000-ton clinker storage silos.

The exit gasses were drawn through the kiln and out of the back end by an induced draught fan. Once exited from the kiln, the gasses would enter electrostatic precipitators. The precipitators were essentially filtration devices that removed the fine dust particles from each of the kilns' exit gasses. This was achieved by passing the gasses between two plates at very high voltages, but very low current. One plate was negatively charged, the other positively charged. This ionized the particles, which, due to electrostatic force, were diverted towards grounded collection plates where they built up and were removed from the gas flow. These particles were then collected in hoppers in the base of the precipitators.

The two modern electrostatic precipitators that were installed in 1991 at a cost of £8 million controlled the dust emissions from the works' 120-meter-tall chimney and helped to give the Westbury works the lowest emission levels since 1992 of any cement works in the United Kingdom. Another benefit of the new precipitators was that the dust particles that were collected could be recycled back into the kilns.

From the storage silos the clinker was then ground with approximately 6 per cent gypsum in one of the four 1,200 hp cement grinding mills. It was essential to add the gypsum at this stage as it controls the setting time of cement; without it, the cement

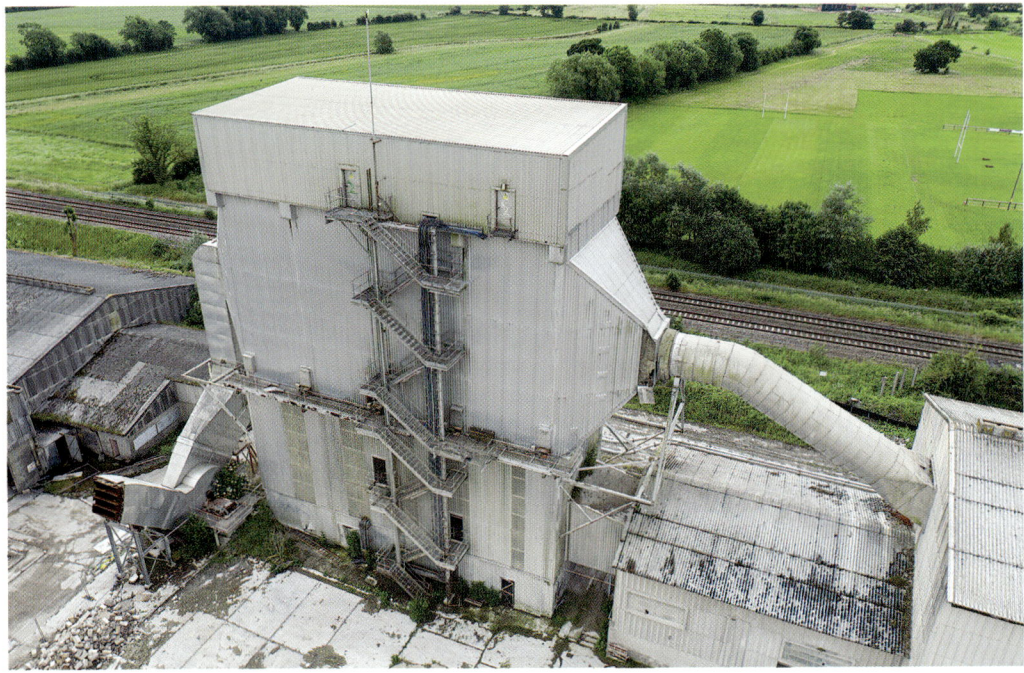

The electrostatic precipitator for Kiln No. 2. The exhaust is still connected to the kiln, but the outlet exhaust has been disconnected from the chimney. 18 June 2016.

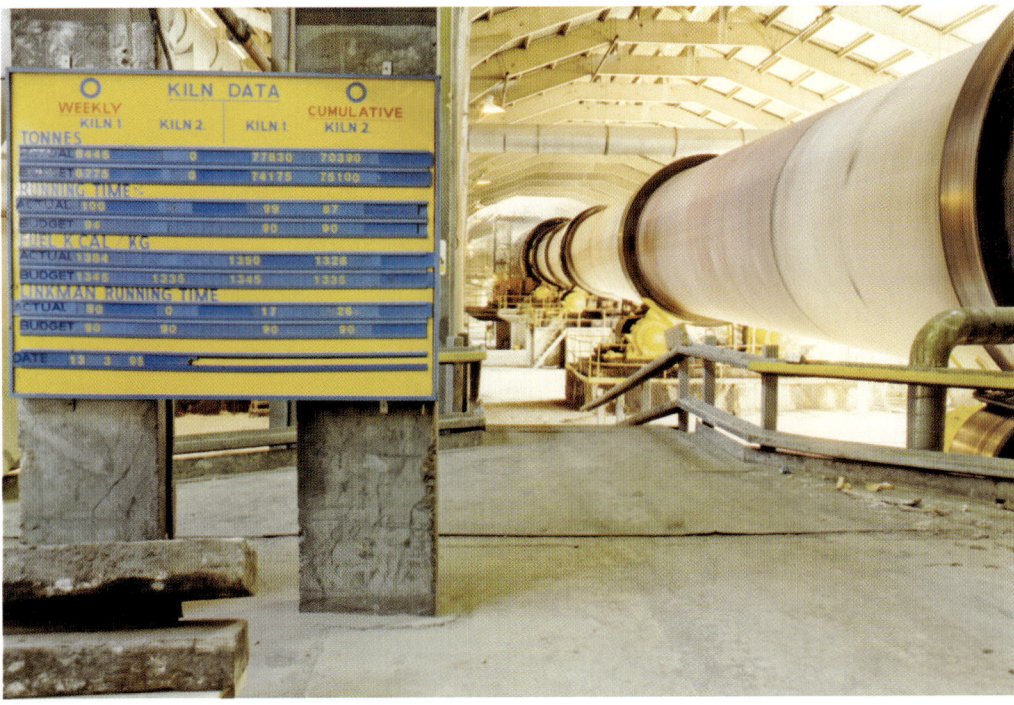

Kiln No. 2 running in 1995. The board is displaying the kiln data for that day. (Courtesy Tarmac Ltd)

The Raw Materials Required in the Production of Cement

would stiffen too quickly and would be impossible to work. Each cylindrical grinding mill rotated on its axis and contained steel media balls. As the mill rotated, it caused the media balls to tumble, which crushed and ground the clinker. The resulting product from the grinding process is cement that started its life as chalk and clay deposits that were millions of years old.

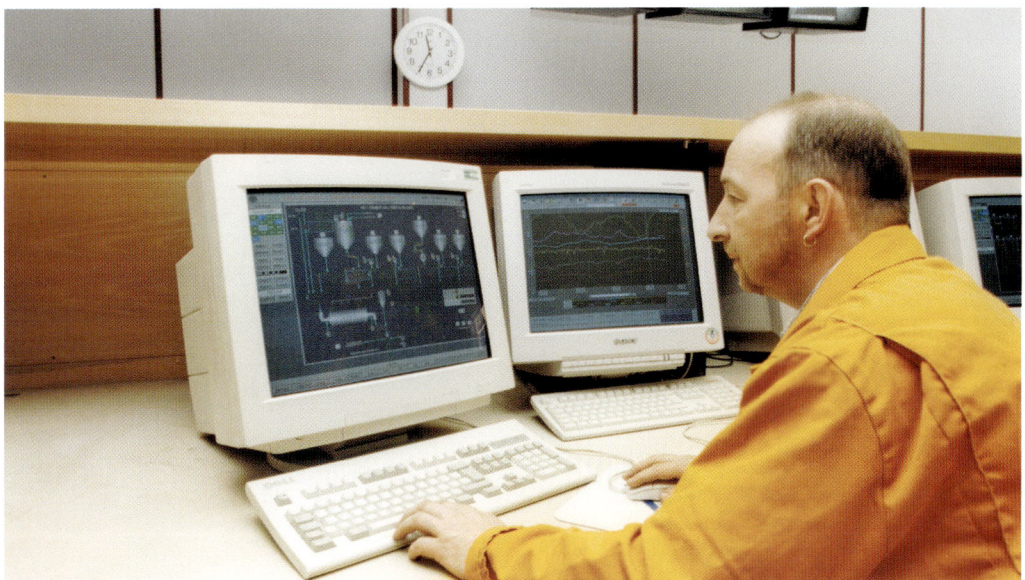

Above: This employee is monitoring the silos and grinding mill.

Right: Here you can see the different sized media balls that were used in the grinding mills. They are being collected by a magnet, to be taken off site.
23 January 2017.

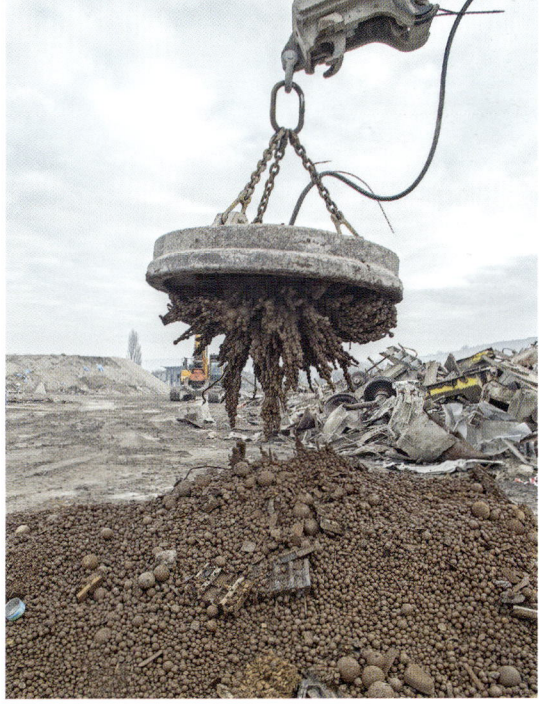

Outlets in the cement mill allowed the cement to be pumped into one of eight 2,000-ton-capacity cement storage silos. From here it would be either transferred to the bulk handling plant to be dispatched by road, or to the packing plant, where it is put into bags via a thirteen-spout packer. This packer is capable of producing bagged cement at a quantity in excess of 100 tons per hour. This very last process – with the cement in the storage silos then moving on to the bulk handling plant or the packing plant – is all that remains of the whole process at the works today.

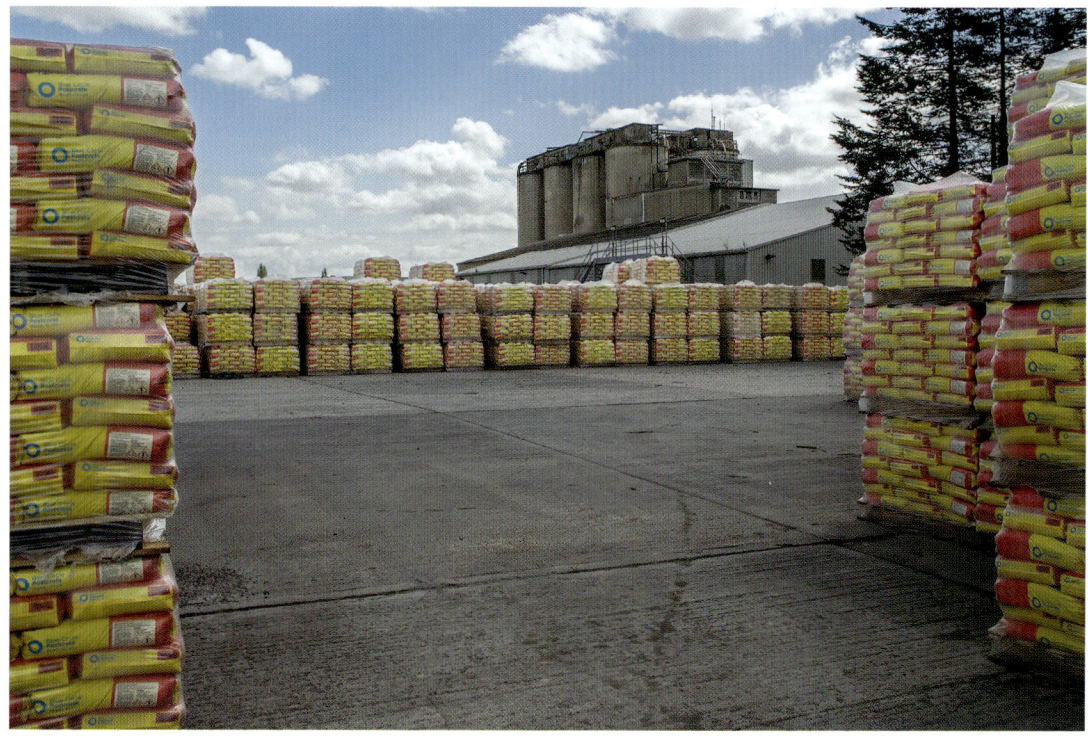

Pallets of Postcrete ready for collection. The packing plant and storage silos are beyond the pallets.

Chapter 5

Kiln and Chimney Construction

The main construction of the works started in 1961, after the access road and rail sidings had been laid in the late 1940s. When the works initially opened, it was operating a single 450-foot rotary kiln that was capable of producing up to 300,000 tons of cement a year.

1964 would see the construction start of a second, taller chimney that would be able to handle the emissions from two kilns. For around eight months, the Westbury skyline was dominated by two tall chimneys, and by June of 1964 the new 120-meter-tall chimney towered over its older counterpart. The first chimney was demolished around October 1965, by which time the new chimney was handling the emissions from both of the original kiln and the newly constructed 500-foot Kiln No. 2. This gave the works

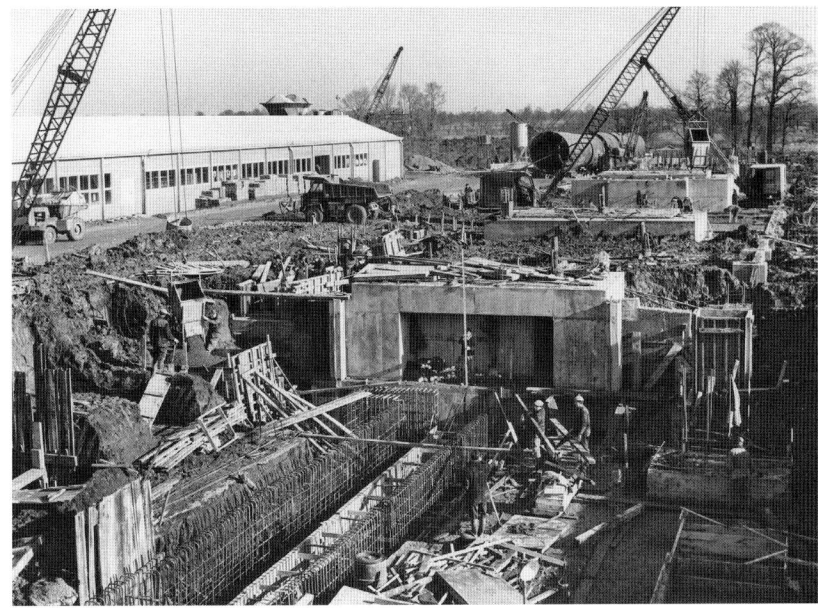

The first stages of construction of Kiln No. 1. In the foreground is the cooler pit area. 8 February 1962.

the capacity produce up to 700,000 tons of cement per year. If demand required, this amount could be increased to 1 million tons per year by importing cement through a depot installed by Westbury W. B. U. at Southampton. This ensured that Westbury could supply cement during the busiest years of any economic cycle.

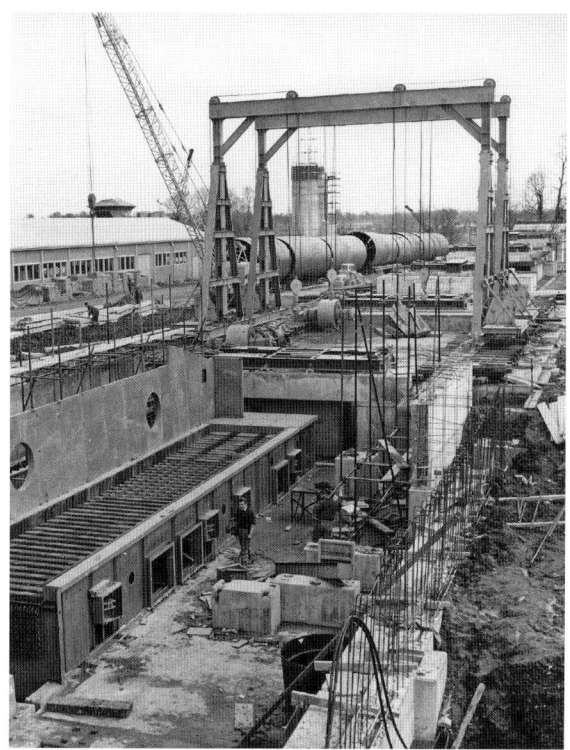

Left: The moving grate cooler is now in place as support rollers and kiln sections await installation. Chimney construction is well underway in the background. 9 April 1962.

Below: The first sections of the kiln are in place, as are all seven piers. 8 May 1962.

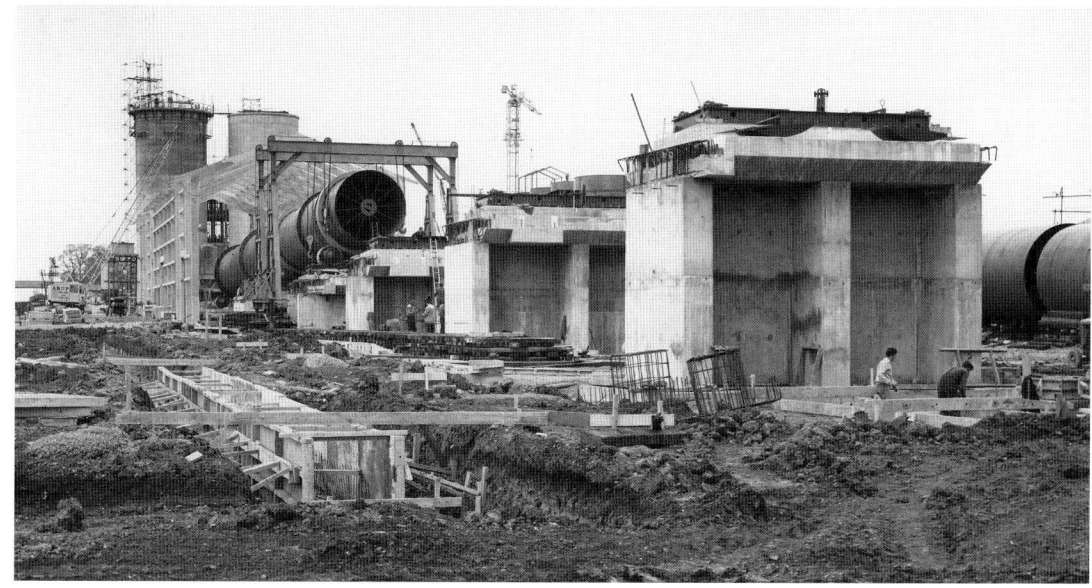

Kiln and Chimney Construction

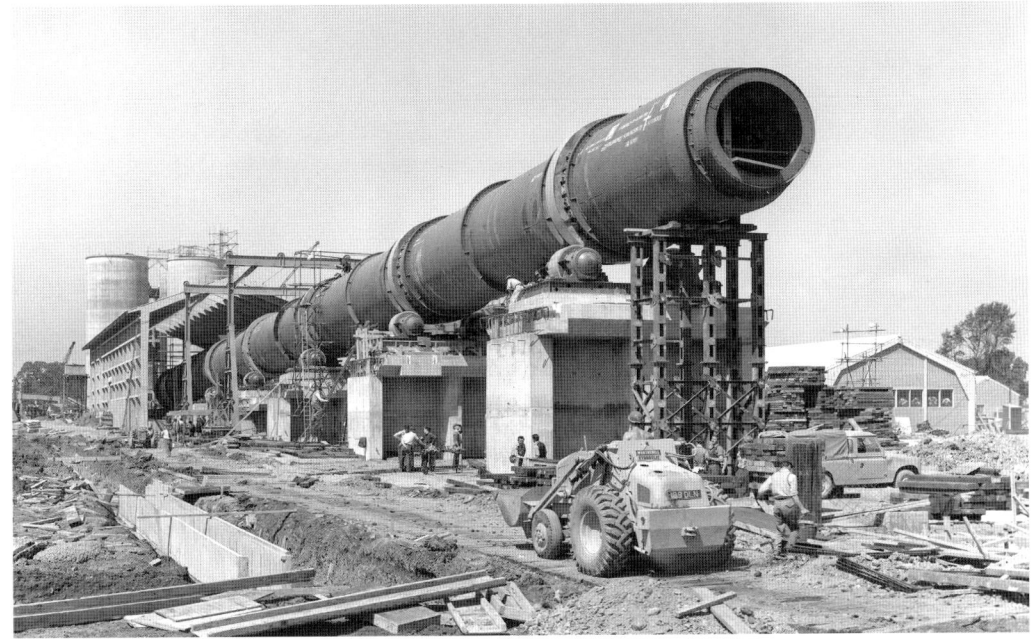

With all sections in place, the 'wet' or back end of the kiln is being supported prior to the installation of the exhaust ducting. 6 June 1962.

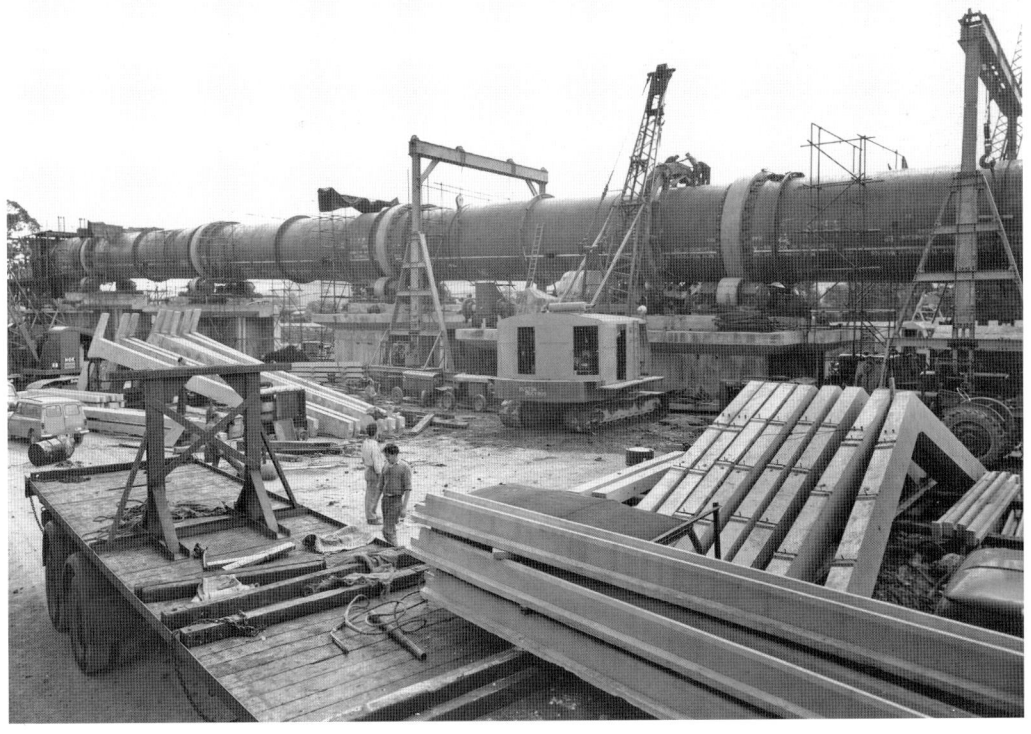

The two-piece drive gear being installed. 8 August 1962.

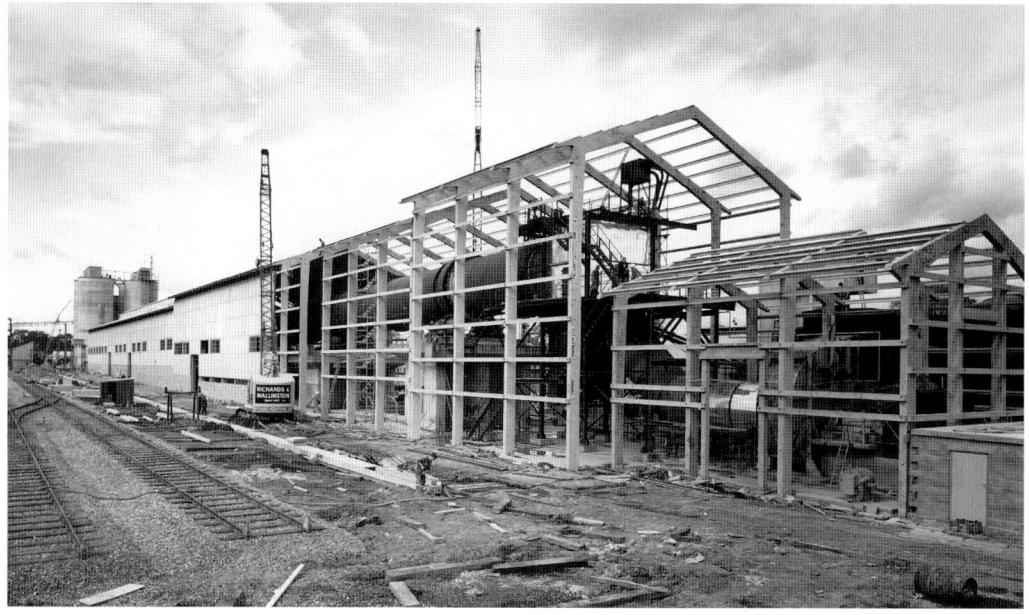

The exhaust ducting is fitted and the kiln building nears completion. The framework of the building bears its maker's name – 'Tarmac Vinculum Precast Concrete'. Blue Circle was taken over by Lafarge, and in 2013 Lafarge became a joint venture with Tarmac, so the company that helped build the works now owns it. 27 September 1962.

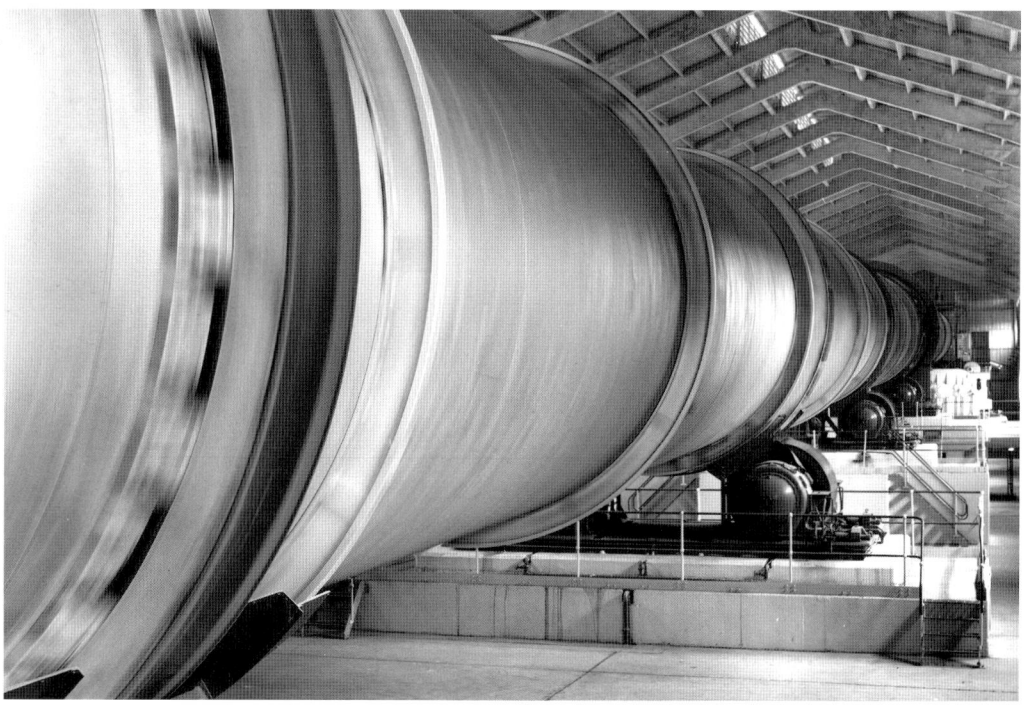

Kiln No. 1 operating at around 1.2 revolutions per minute. 29 April 1963.

Kiln and Chimney Construction

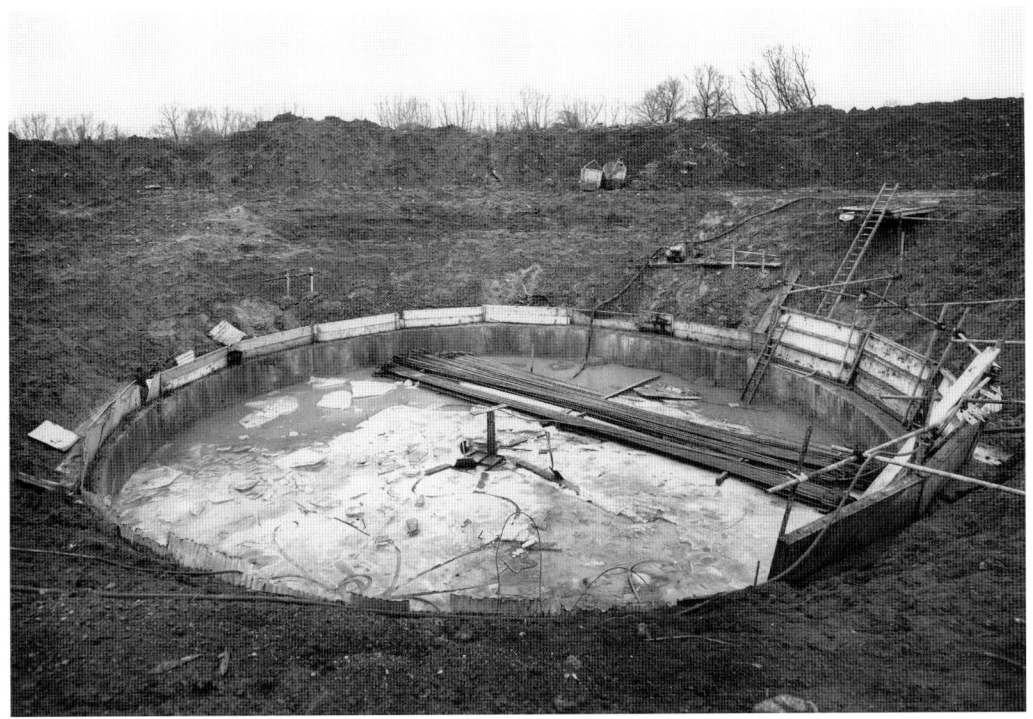

Above: The foundations for the first chimney. The ice highlights that 1962 was one of the coldest winters on record – it was also known as 'The Big Freeze'. 8 January 1962.

Right: Piles of insulating bricks wait to line the interior of the new chimney. 9 April 1962.

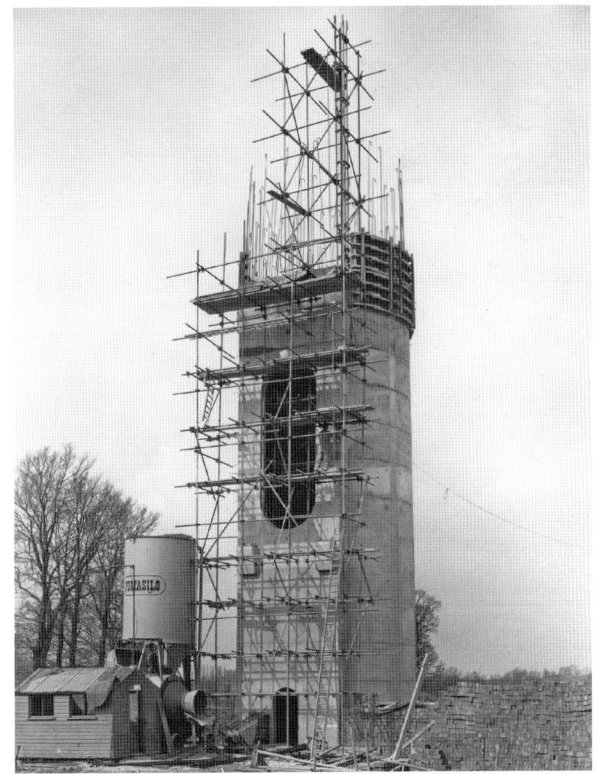

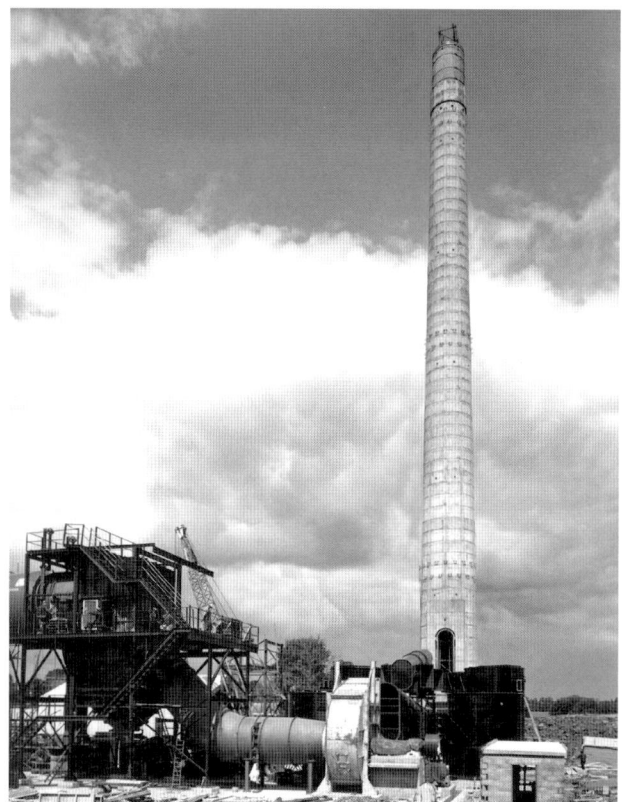

Left: The fan that helps pull air through the kiln and to the chimney is in the foreground and the new chimney is complete. 8 August 1962.

Below: The cooler pit area of Kiln No. 2. The hot clinker would travel along the area of the central trench and would then head off to the left via a bucket conveyor to the storage silos. 6 November 1964.

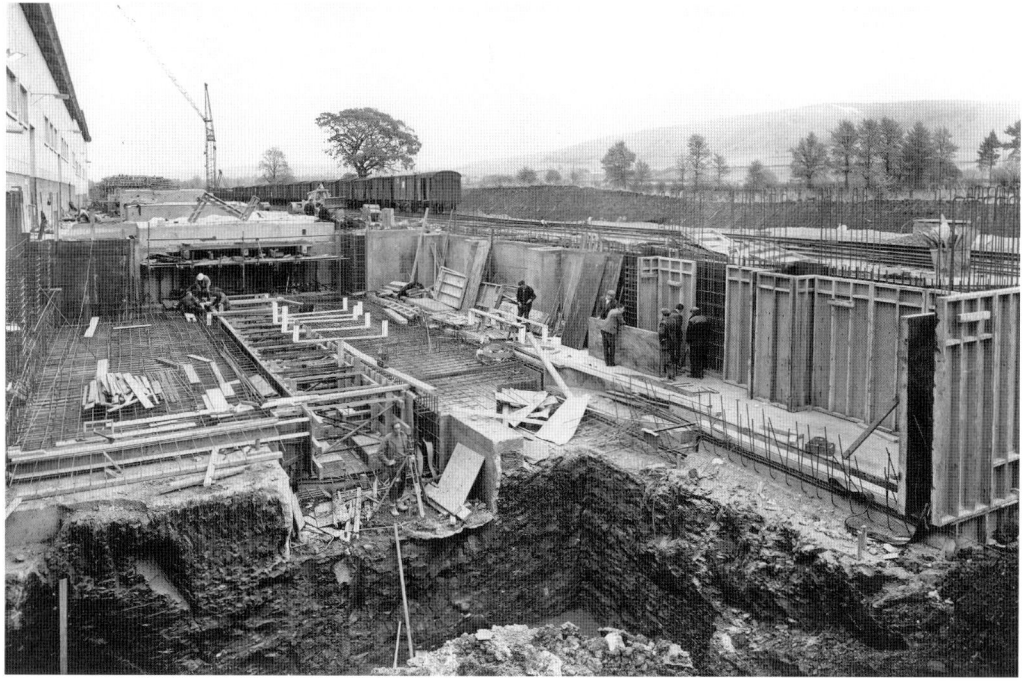

Kiln and Chimney Construction

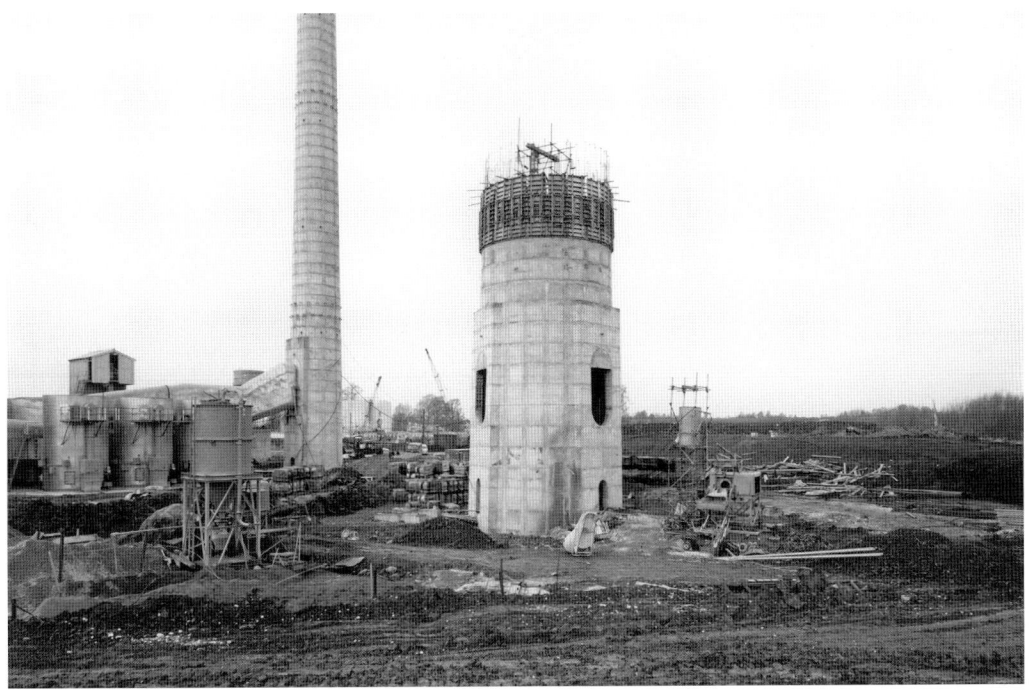

Above: Construction of the second chimney. 7 December 1964.

Right: The structure around the top of the chimney is a circular formwork that climbs the chimney each time another lift of concrete is cast. 5 February 1965.

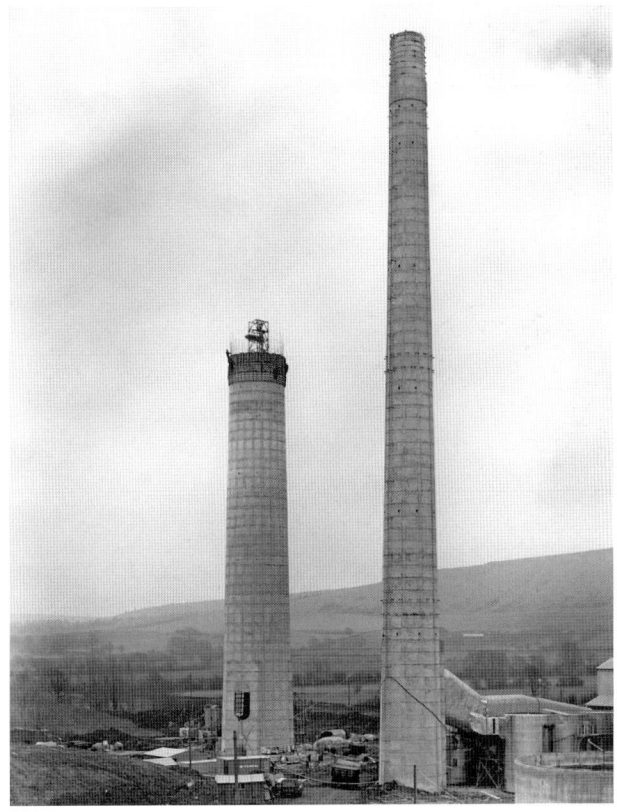

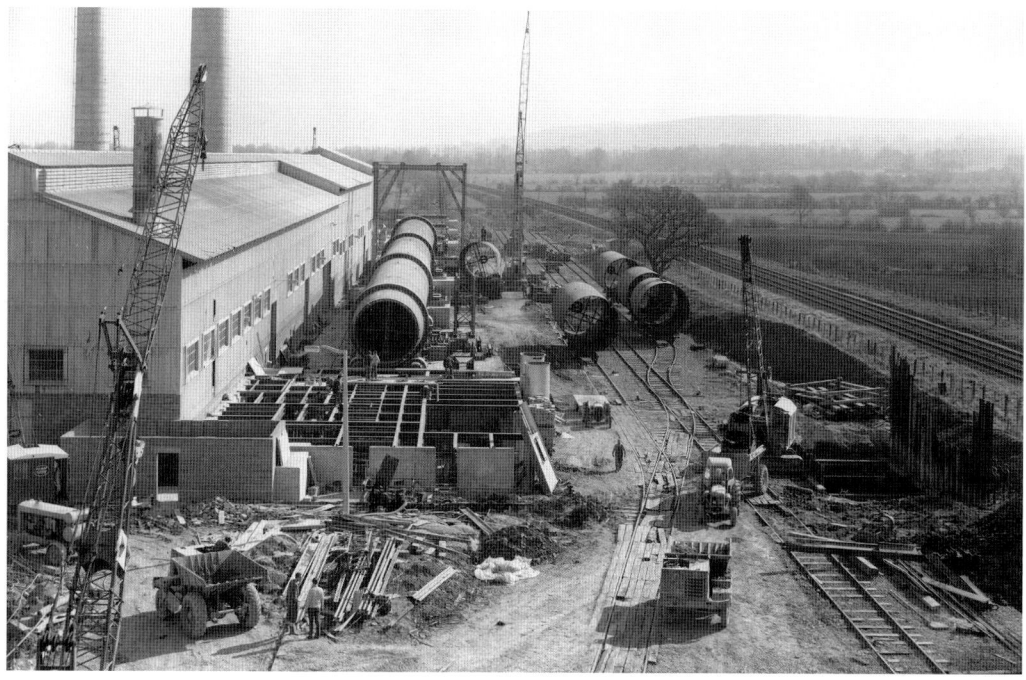

The internal bracing that was used for transport and installation can be seen in the kiln sections yet to be installed. 1 April 1965.

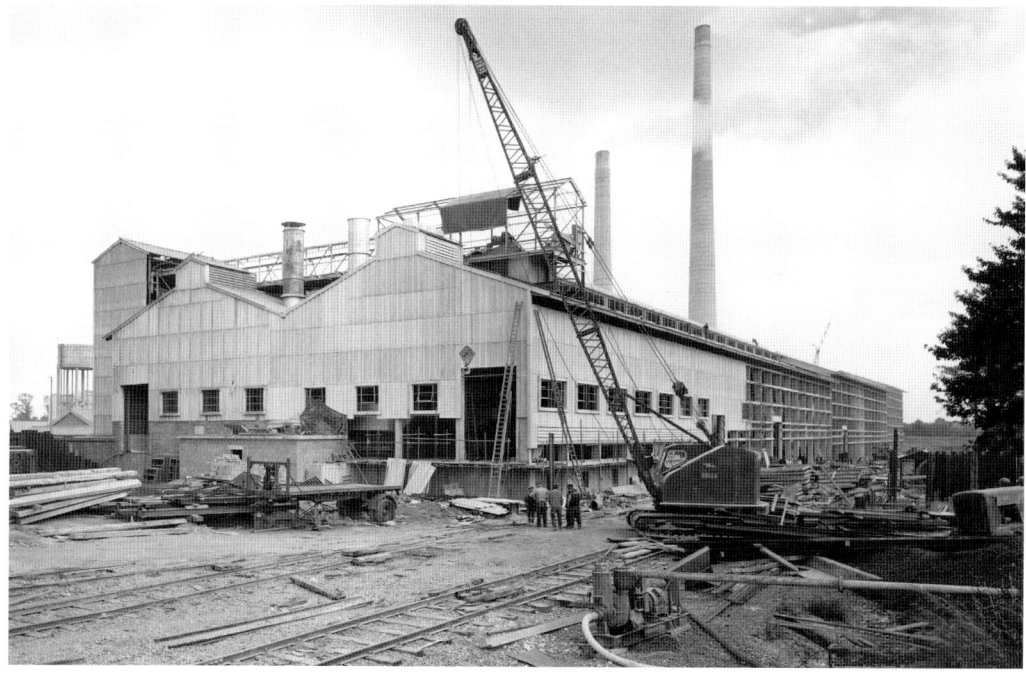

Kiln No. 2 is running, as is evident from the smoke coming from both chimneys. Within three months the new chimney would be handling the emissions from both kilns. 7 July 1965.

Kiln and Chimney Construction

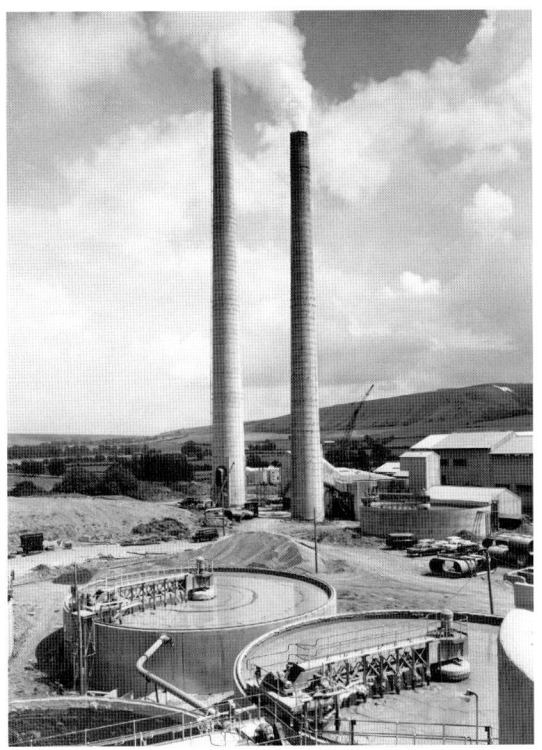

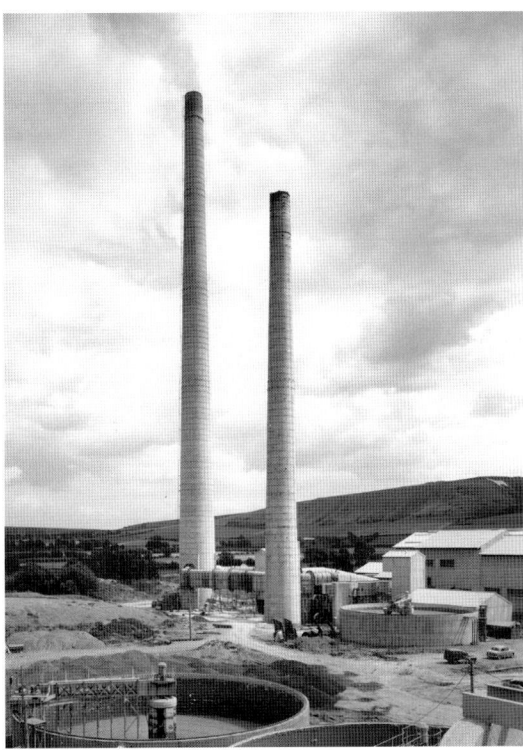

Above left: One of the very few pictures that exist of both chimneys in operation. The slurry mixers are in the foreground. 7 July 1965.

Above right: The new chimney is now handling the emissions from the kilns, with the exhaust ducting having been removed from the original chimney. 9 August 1965.

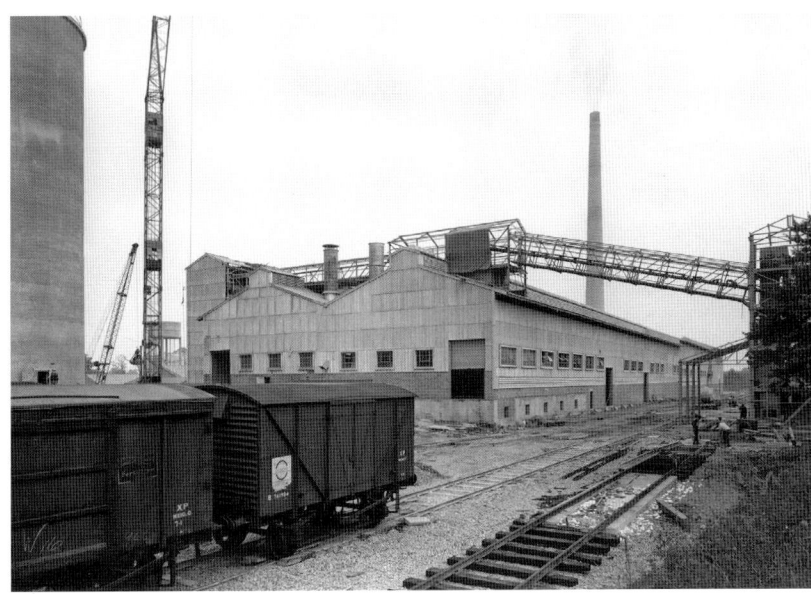

The new kiln building is finished as work on the coal elevator and conveyor that delivered coal to the kilns nears completion. 7 October 1965.

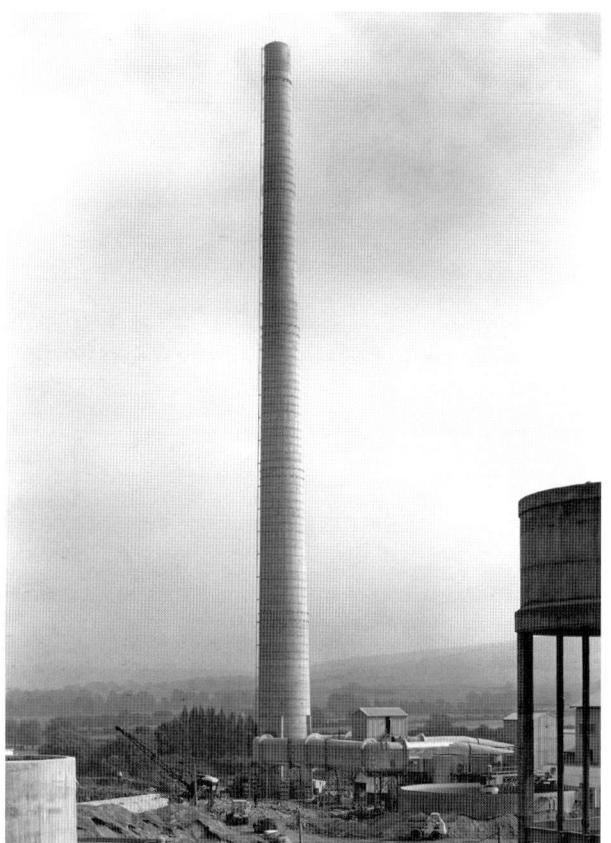

Left: Now the view that most are familiar with. In the bottom left corner of the picture the concrete remains of the first chimney lie on the ground, being demolished by a machine with a wrecking ball. 7 October 1965.

Below: The new kiln building and the very small (by 1991 standards) precipitators. 3 November 1965.

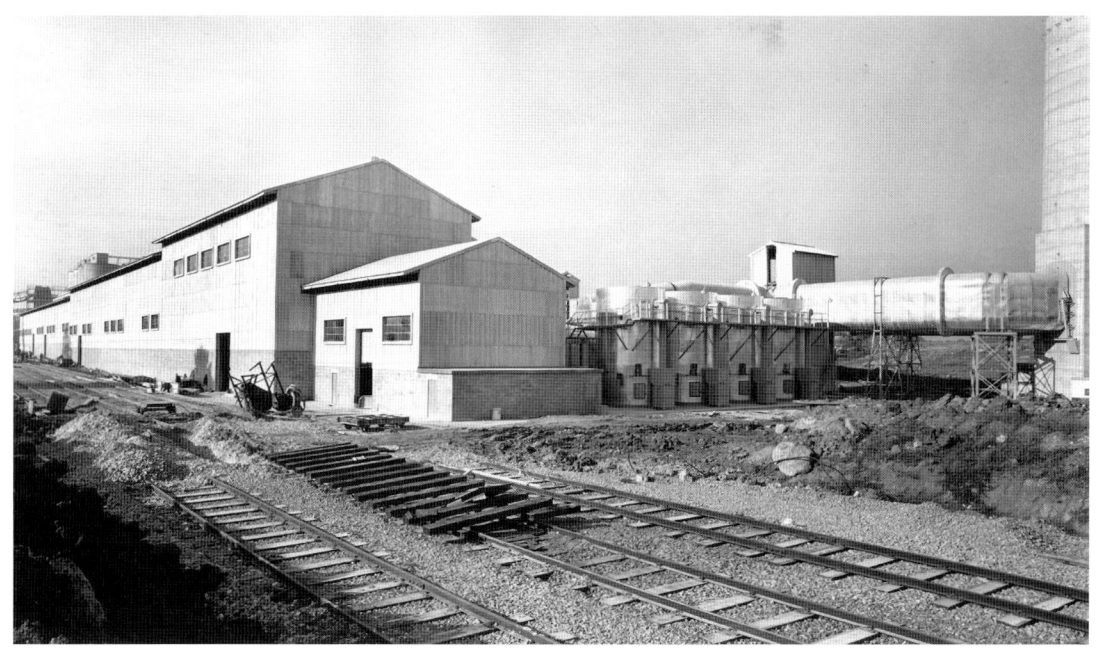

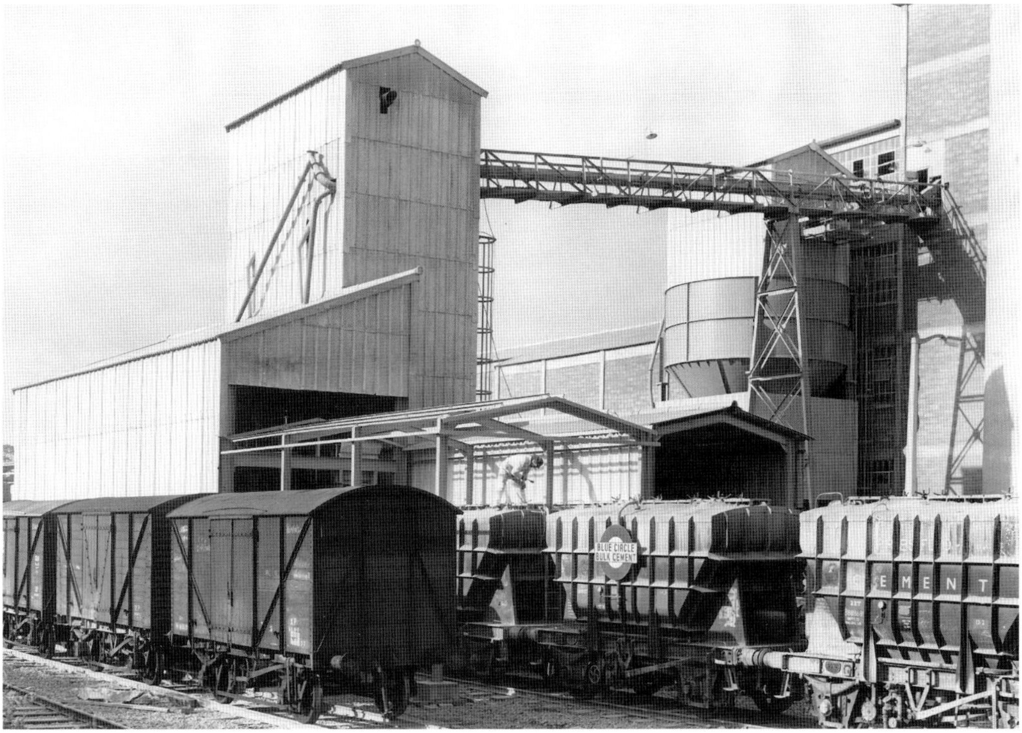

Kiln and Chimney Construction

The rail bulk loading bay. 3 November 1965.

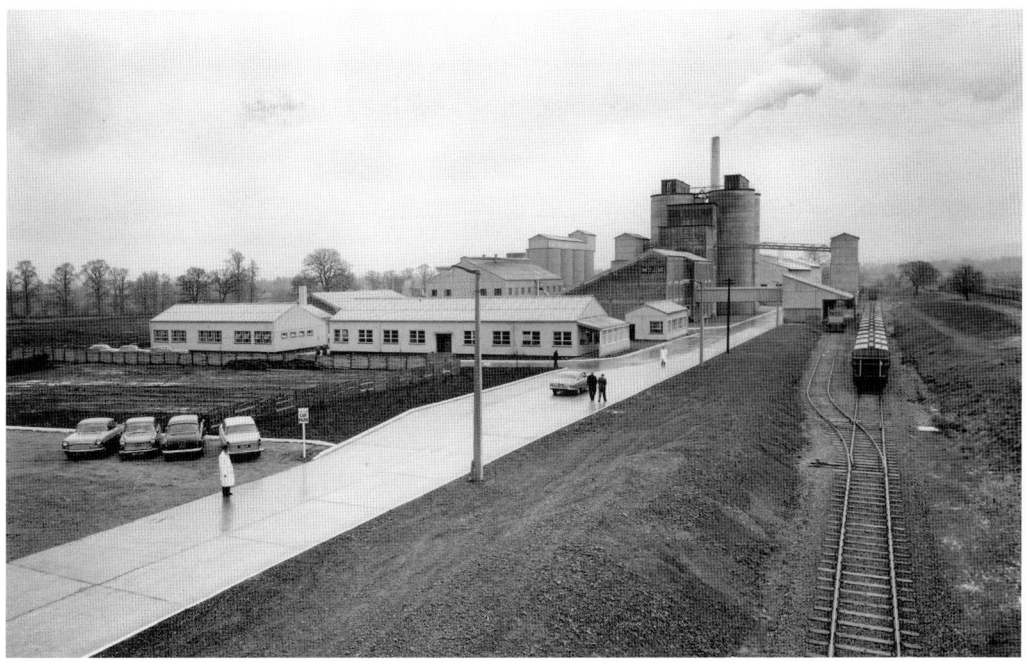

The railway siding. 29 April 1963.

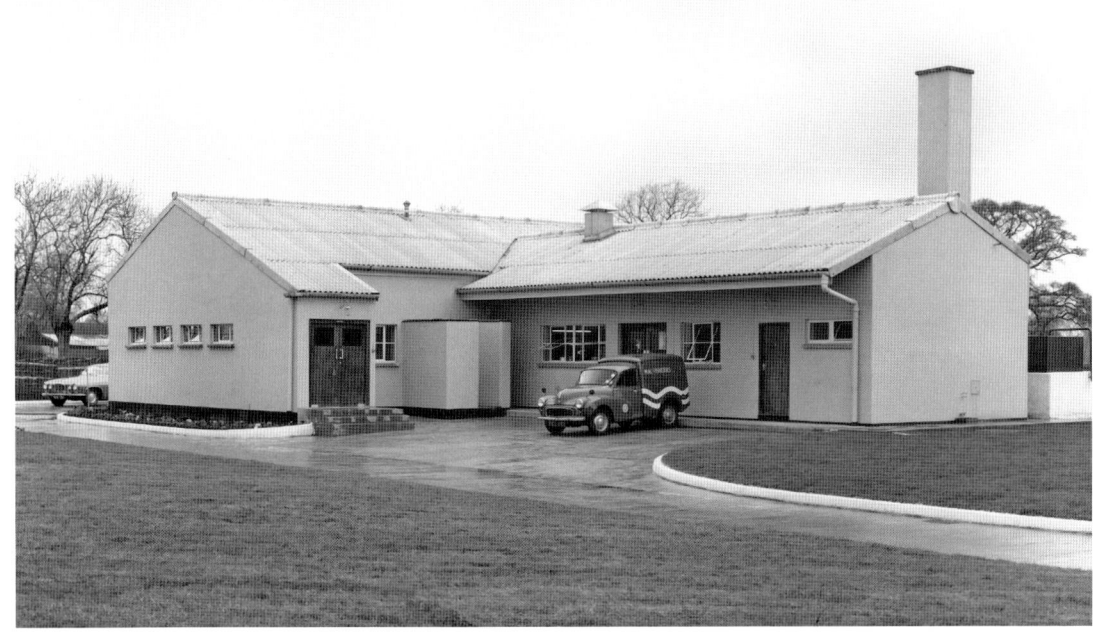

The canteen. 29 April 1963.

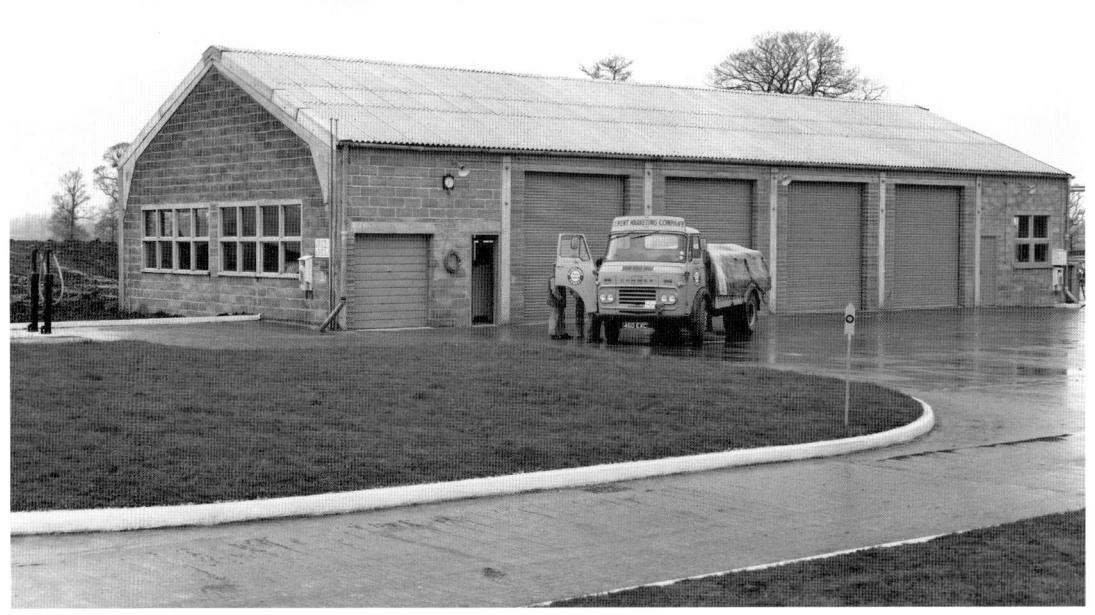

The garage building. 29 April 1963.

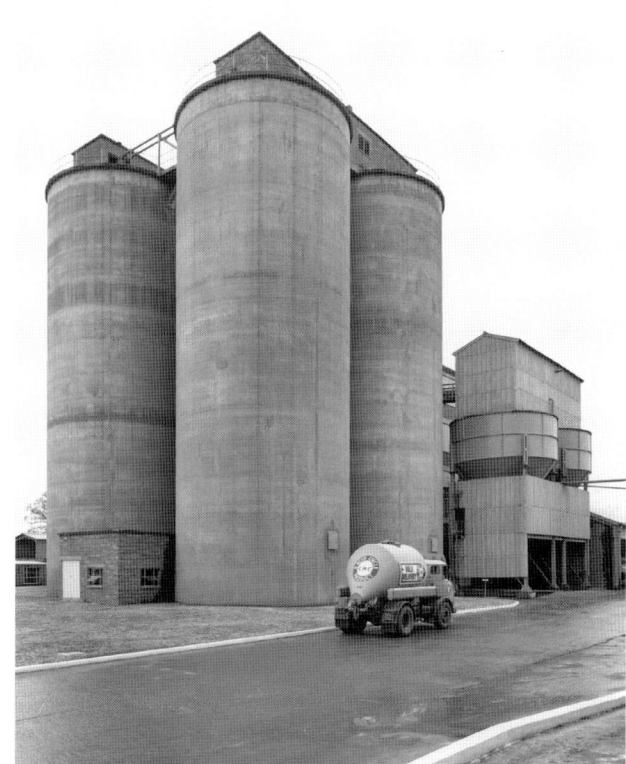

Right: The bulk loading and cement silos. Four more silos would be added in the future to cope with the increased production from two kilns. 29 April 1963.

Below: The loading bay. 29 April 1963.

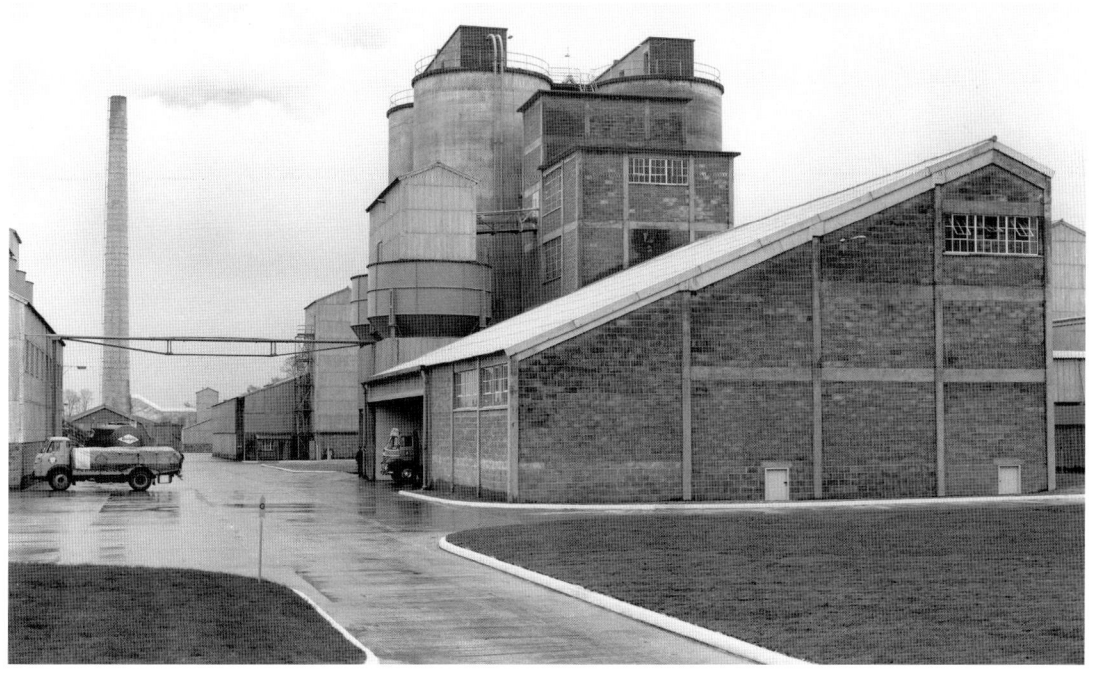

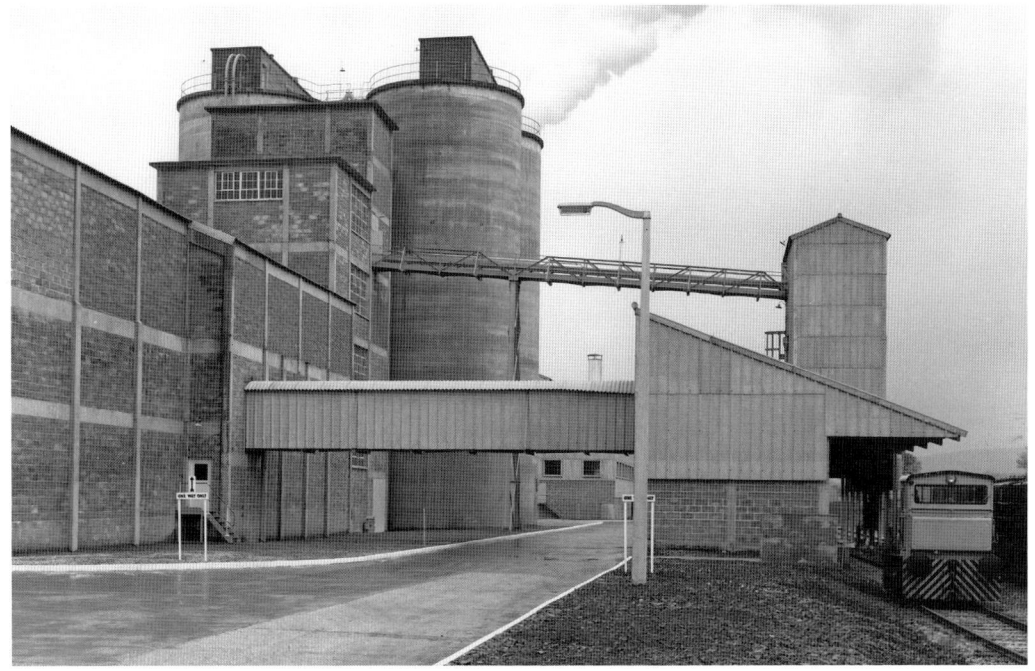

The back end of the loading bay. 29 April 1963.

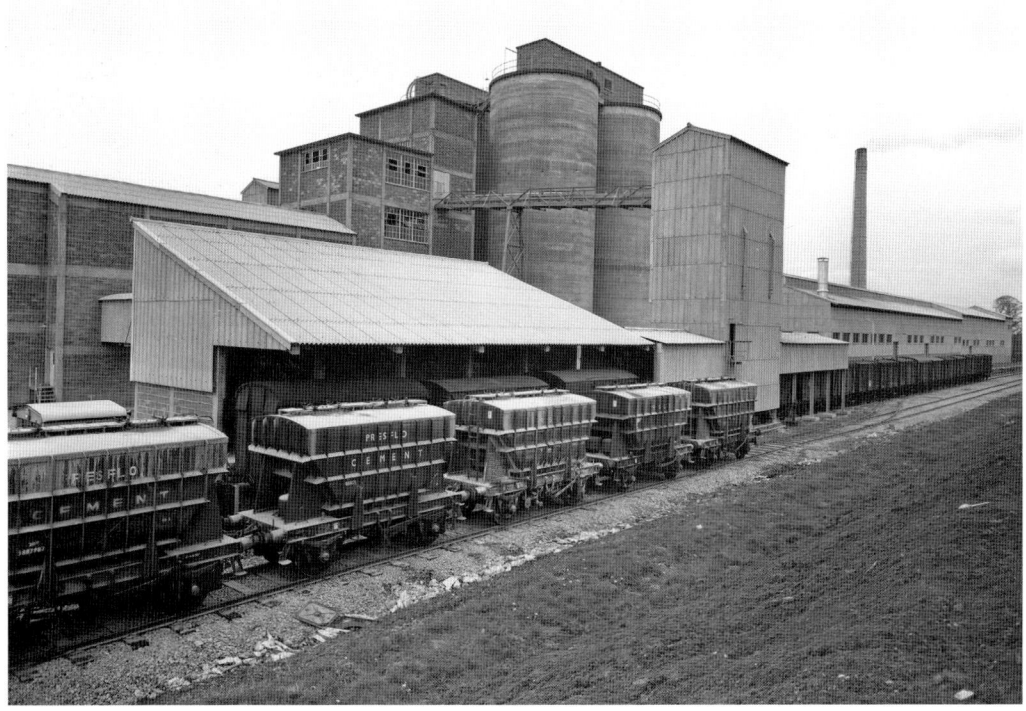

The rail bulk loading bay. 29 April 1963.

Kiln and Chimney Construction

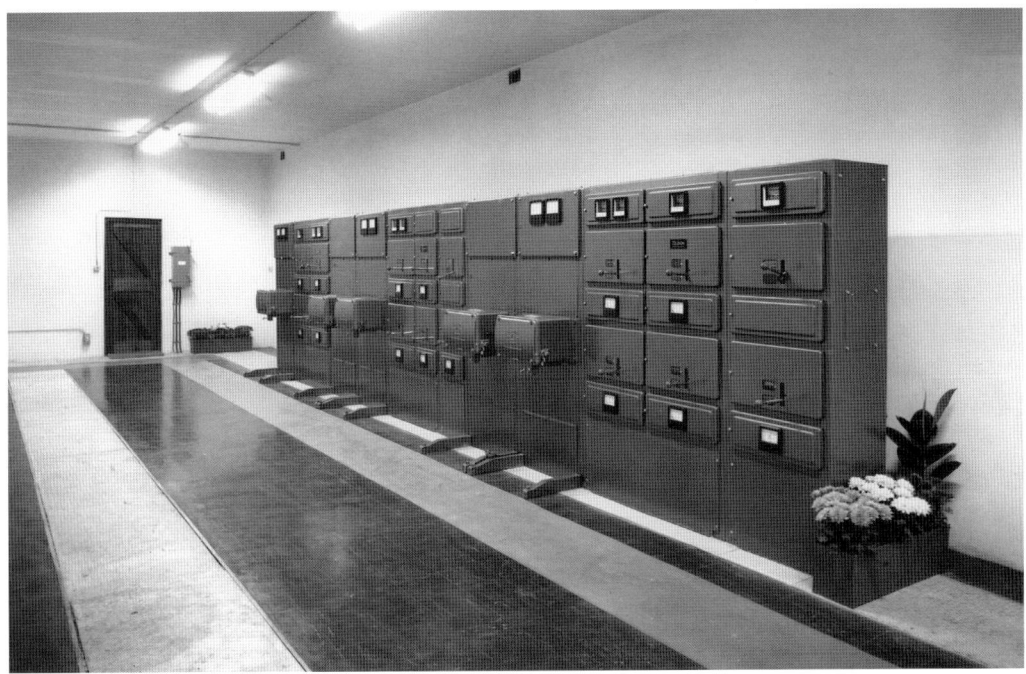

The low voltage switch gear in the power house. 29 April 1963.

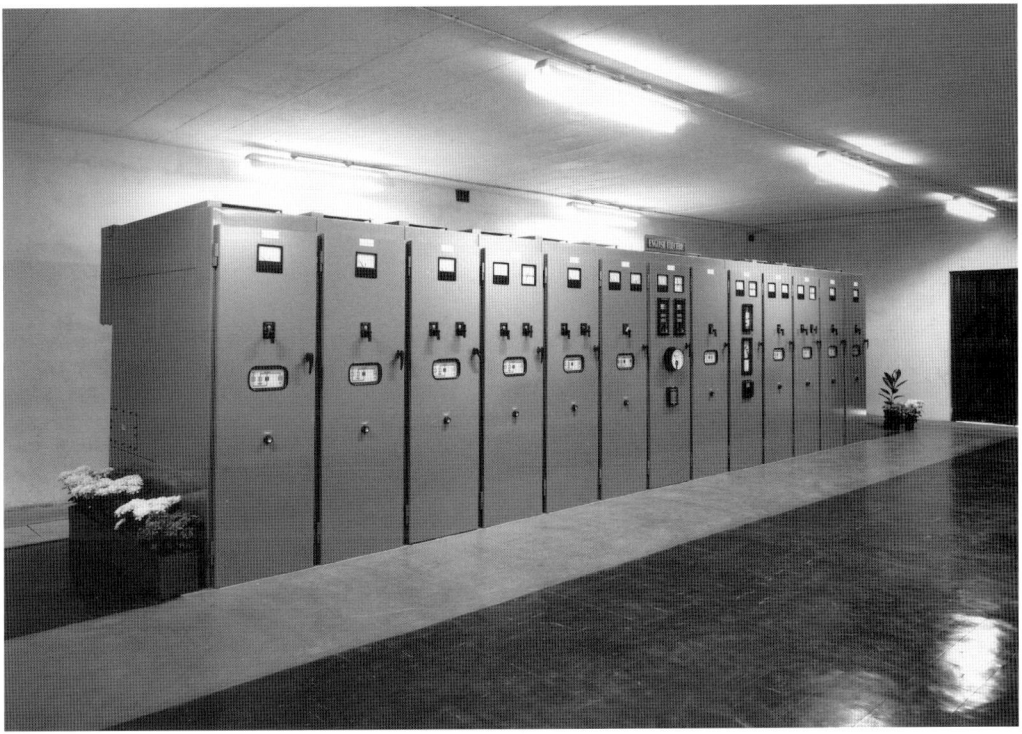

The high voltage switch gear. 29 April 1963.

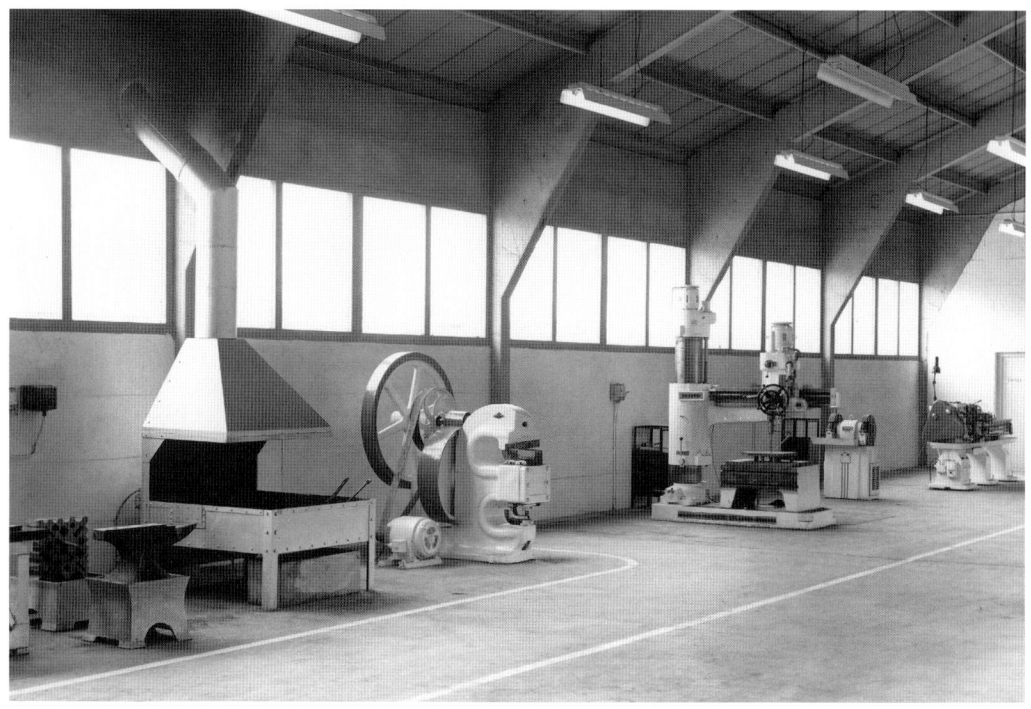

The fitting shop, with a forge closest on the left, a grinder and a radial arm drill. 29 April 1963.

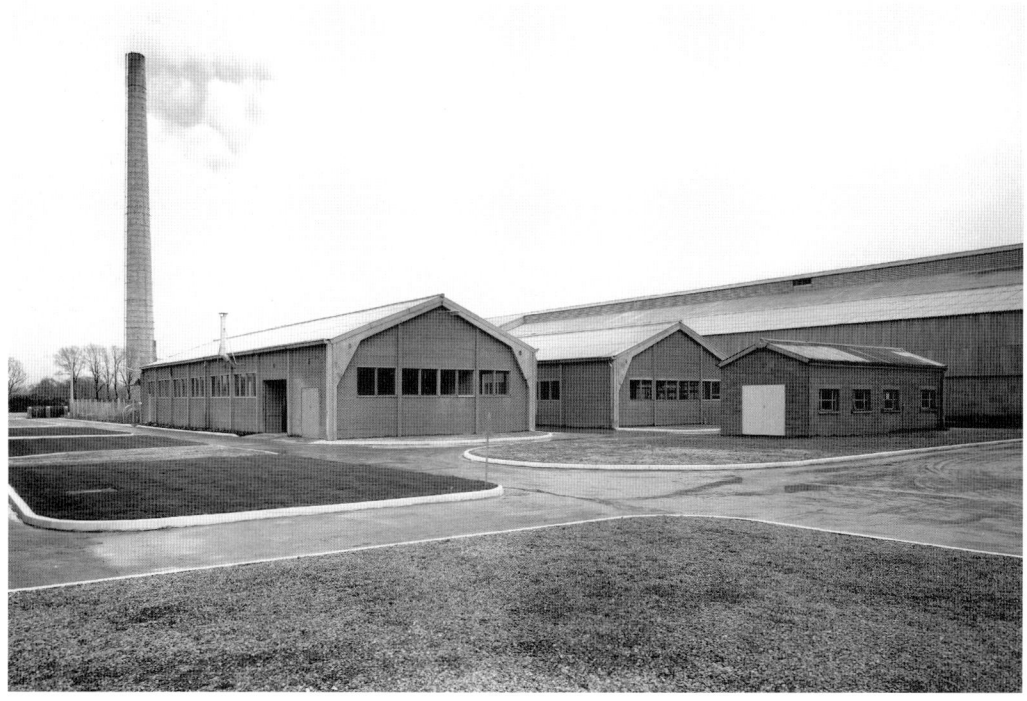

The stores and fitting shop area. 29 April 1963.

Kiln and Chimney Construction

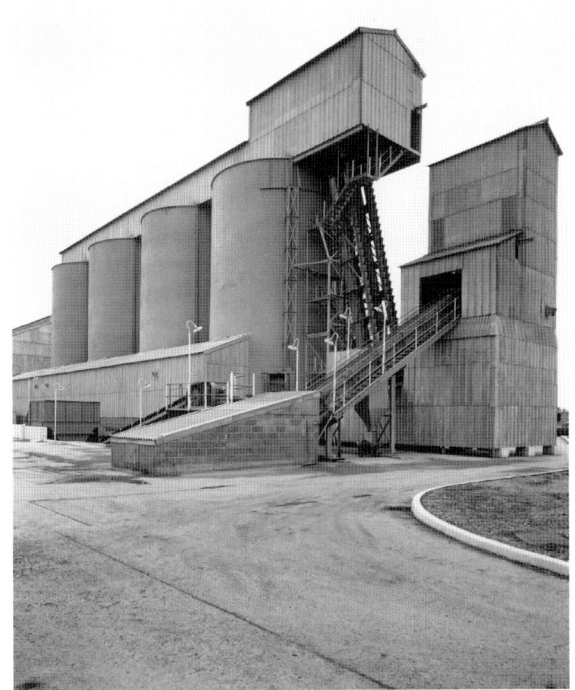

Right: The clinker and gypsum silos and conveyors. 29 April 1963.

Below: Four more clinker silos have now been added to cope with increased kiln output. 15 December 1965.

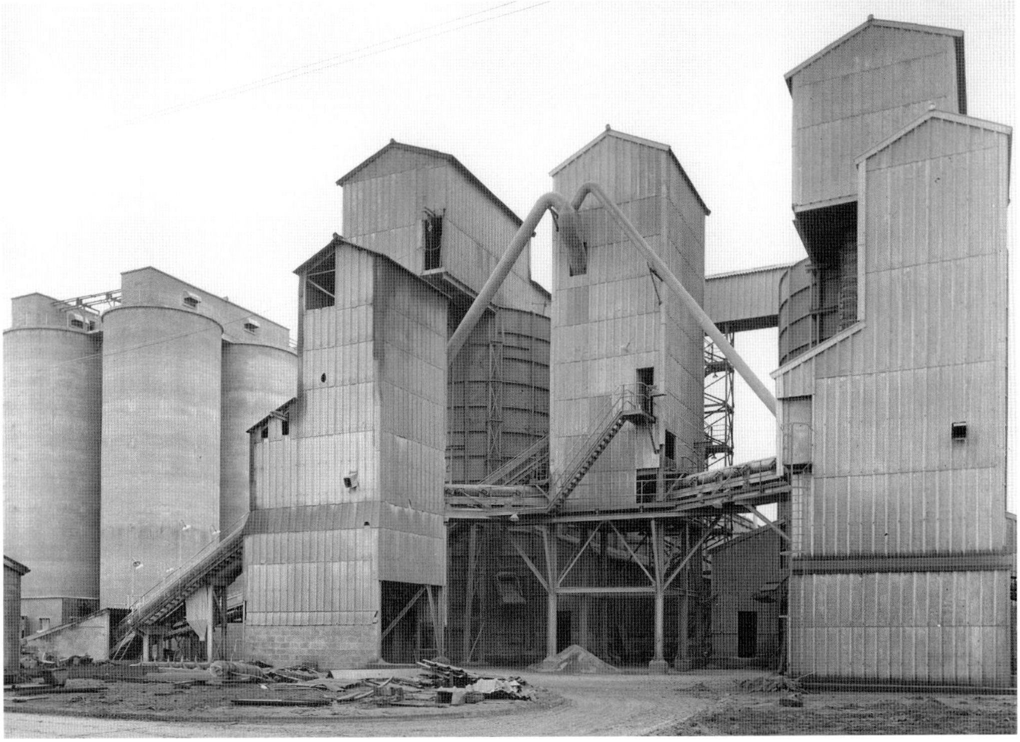

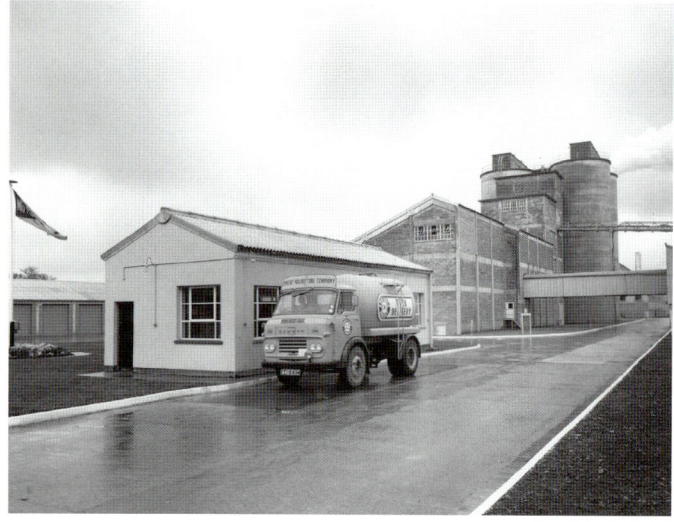

A Commer cement lorry waiting on the weighbridge. 29 April 1963.

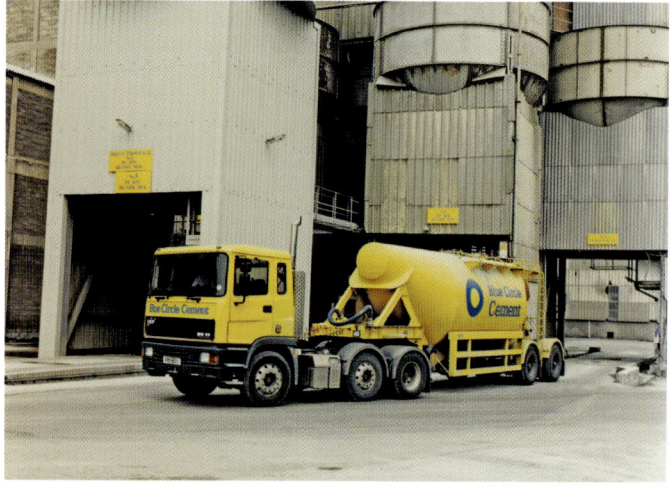

A Blue Circle Cement lorry waiting to take its load off site.

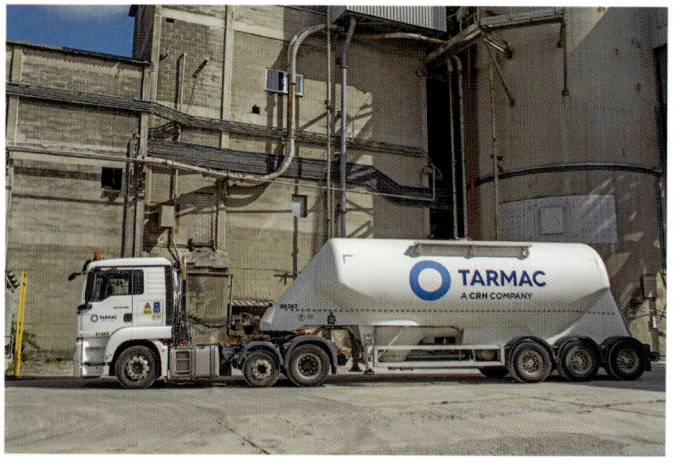

A present-day Tarmac cement lorry carrying the Blue Circle logo after the 2013 merger.

Kiln and Chimney Construction

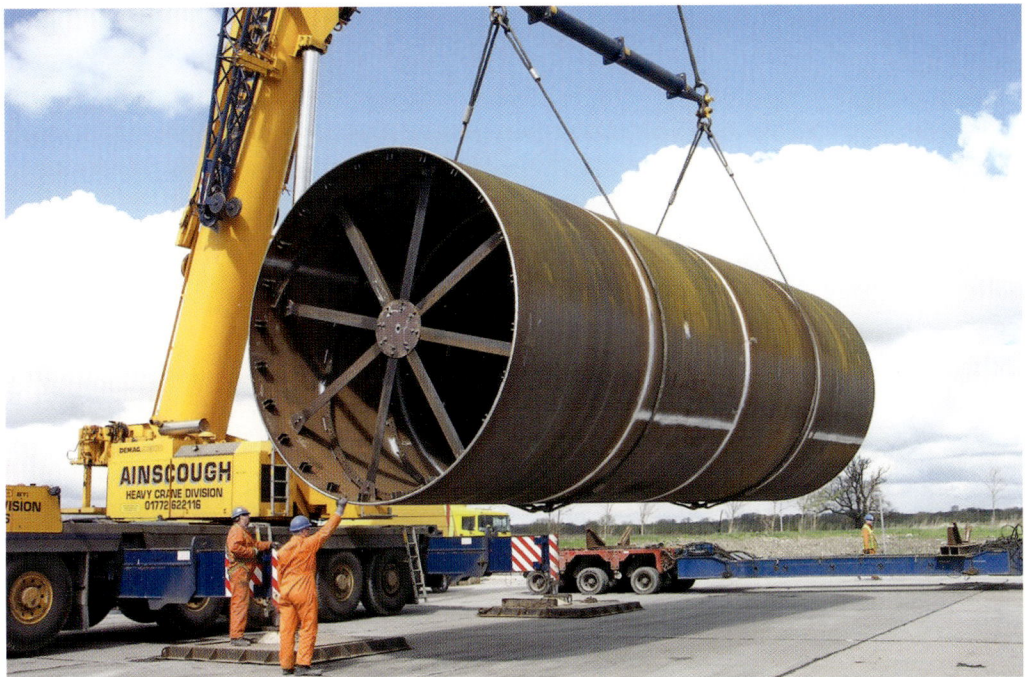

Above: A replacement kiln section being delivered in 2006. (Courtesy Tarmac Ltd)

Right: The kilns' lining of insulating firebricks being replaced. To assess wear on the bricks, they were drilled through and the depth of the brick was measured. Later, when the technology became available, brick depth was measured with radar. (Courtesy Tarmac Ltd)

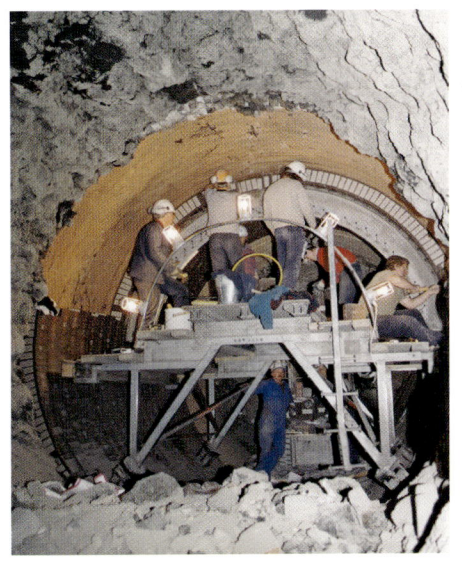

In 2001 Blue Circle Industries was taken over by Lafarge Cement and the combination of these two firms created the world's largest cement producer. At this time, demand for cement was very high and Kilns Nos 1 and 2 were fully employed. During this period the only planned shutdown of the kilns was for maintenance.

During periods of lower demand, Kiln No. 1 would be shut down. Unfortunately, as recession hit the country in 2008, demand for cement dropped off dramatically, and kiln No.1 was shut down for good. Less than a year later, Kiln No. 2 followed suit.

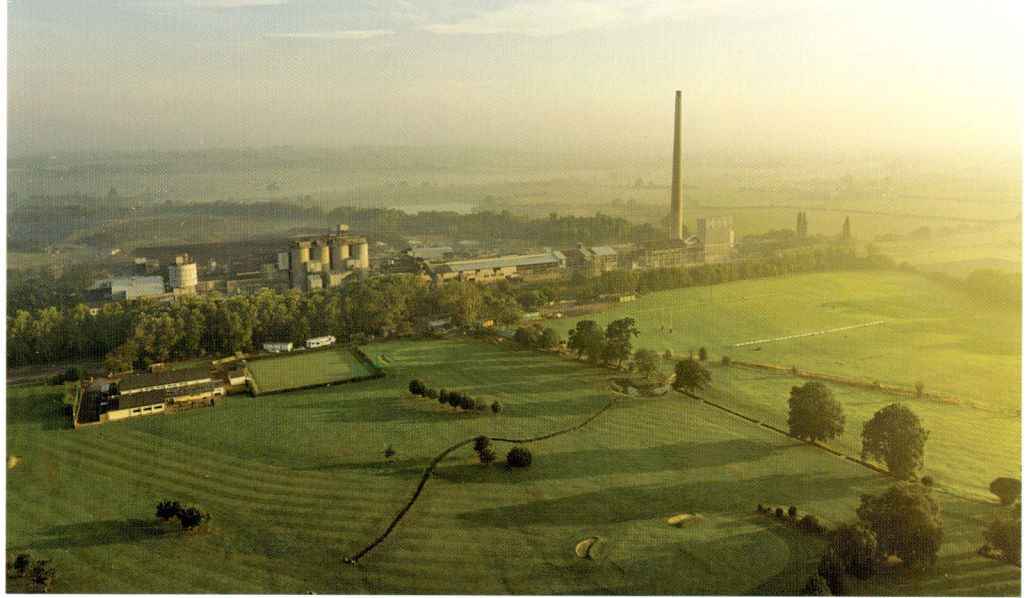

The golf course, club house, bowling green and rugby club. 14 September 2016.

Employees

At its peak, the works provided employment for a workforce of around 200 that oversaw the 24-hours-a-day, seven-days-a-week operation of the works. It was therefore a major employer in the Westbury area.

A company is nothing without its employees and Blue Circle understood this simple fact. The company valued the safety, welfare and the social aspects of working life and a committee was set up that comprised both management and employee representatives. This ensured the values that the company held, and all aspects of works operation could be discussed fairly.

To help build a thriving social environment at the works, a social club was built within the grounds. It opened in 1970 and provided a base for a wide range of activities that included football, cricket, bowls, badminton, skittles, snooker, dancing, rifle shooting, fishing, photography and even gardening. Employees also built their own nine-hole golf course. To help support these recreational sections, weekly contributions by Blue Circle and its employees were made to a welfare fund.

Blue Circle would also provide inter-works games for football, cricket, bowls and golf that were held in the London Borough of Bromley. Snooker exhibitions were held at the Westbury works' social club, with players such as Cliff Wilson, Jimmy White and Alex Higgins gracing the club's tables.

August Bank Holidays would always bring the works families together when the social club would host various forms of entertainment, both indoors and out. Two welfare employees – Maurice Barker and Trish Selby – both worked hard to make the family days successful. Another popular family event would be an annual works outing to places such as Alton Towers and Chessington World of Adventures.

The welfare AGM was another event that the workers looked forward to, where a lavish meal would be laid on at the social club.

Christmas was a magical time for the children of the works employees. George Poole would take on his role as Father Christmas and the social club would become Santa's Grotto, where the children would get to meet and receive presents from Santa.

All of the efforts Blue Circle and the works employees put into the welfare and social aspects of working life at the Westbury site helped ensure a strong sense of community, which further strengthened its position as one of the better employers in the local area.

Works Characters

As with any work place, the works has seen its fair share of characters over the years, many of whom spent most of their working lives at the Westbury works. Sadly, some are no longer with us now. Below are just a few memories and stories about some of these characters.

One such character was Trevor Heeks. Trevor would practice his town crier shout against the noise of the cement mills – and it paid off. Trevor has won numerous town crying competitions, and at the time of writing has been Trowbridge town crier for more than thirty years.

One day an employee decided to take the Barford dumper to The Duke in works time. He had a pint and then went shopping, only to be confronted by Harold Mackley (then works manager) on his return to work and was given instant dismissal. Harold was always there when a kiln went down, wanting men in as soon as possible. On one such occasion he dashed into the kiln and when he came out he stood with his smouldering false leg in a bucket of water, declaring, 'OK, that's fine to go in now lads!'

Percy Daniels, of gypsy origin, was a real character. Percy was always cheerful and was often looked upon with some amusement. He was responsible for the upkeep of the lavatories and always contributed to the weekly Tote. He could normally be found whistling while working and had a nickname for everybody.

Henry Brooks and Alan Vanderplank, who was a bit of an artist, would always be seen wearing wellington boots.

George Poole, the yard foreman, was prominent and forthright. He was a member of the local fox hunting fraternity, and when he was buried a bugler played 'Gone to Ground' at the service.

Will Davies, an intense character, was passionate about nature. He came close to death when he fell into a bottle well while out walking with his dog and bird of prey in North Bradley. The bird of prey became agitated by Will's cries for help, which luckily alerted a friend, Trevor Hemmings, who called for assistance. This made the local news!

One day Will was challenged by his work colleagues to see if he could shoot one of the site's numerous pigeons with his air rifle. He accepted this challenge and was soon cooking the unfortunate bird in a pan! He later gained permission to carry out a cull of the pigeons on the works site.

'Stoney' was from Stoney Gutter and hated paying tax, especially at Christmas. Many times, he threatened Ivor Gill through the pay hatch!

Janet Beard ran the works shop for many years, providing hot and cold food and drink, and was very much appreciated.

Chapter 6

A Ghost Town

Walking around the site in 2016, especially when there was no demolition going on, was somewhat eerie. Having never set foot on anything like the site before, I also found it slightly unnerving. Tall buildings and structures towered above, and even though I did know that I was safe, I sometimes felt as if there was some unknown danger waiting to catch me out. In hindsight, this was a good thing as it gave me even more of a healthy respect for the site – which was especially important for when I would later be on site during the demolition.

Some buildings (the labs for example) still had equipment out on the benches. Some offices still had computers and telephones on the desks. Kitchen areas still had kettles, mugs and spoons, and even bottles of ketchup were still left out. It was almost as if there had been an emergency evacuation of the place. There was a locker room with belongings still in the lockers. The locker room would have been somewhere that employees discussed their lives, the shift that they had just finished or the funny thing that someone had done or said. Meeting up for a drink at the Social Club would have been arranged from the locker room. The various stickers, posters and graffiti that adorned the lockers offered a small insight into the various characters that laughed, joked and complained in this room some seven years ago.

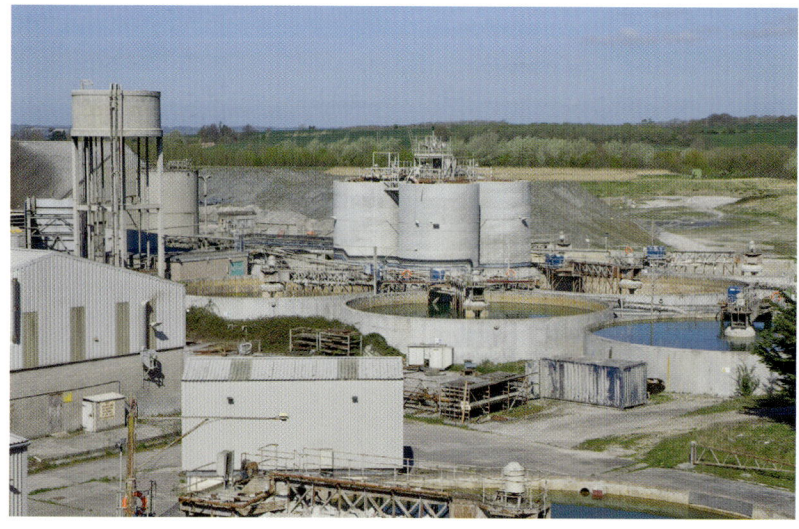

The water tower is on the left, and the three visible doctor tanks are surrounded by water-filled slurry mixers. The diesel pumping station is in the foreground, in front of slurry mixer No. 9. (Copyright Nigel Osman)

A Ghost Town

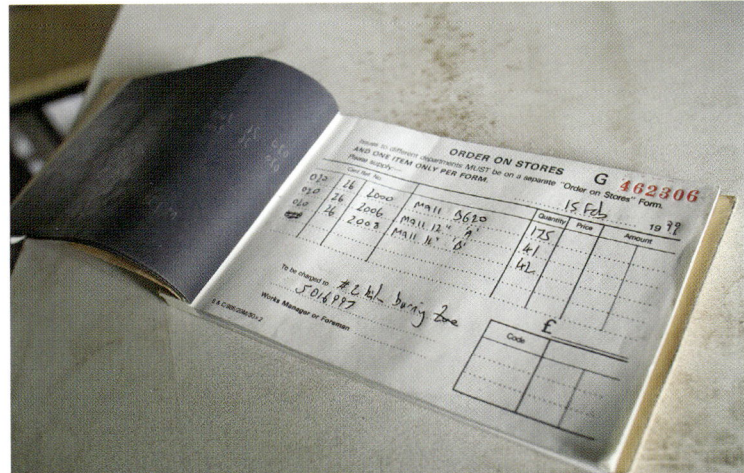

Kiln No. 2 was shut down for maintenance at this time and the order was for bricks in the burning zone of the kiln. 15 February 1999.

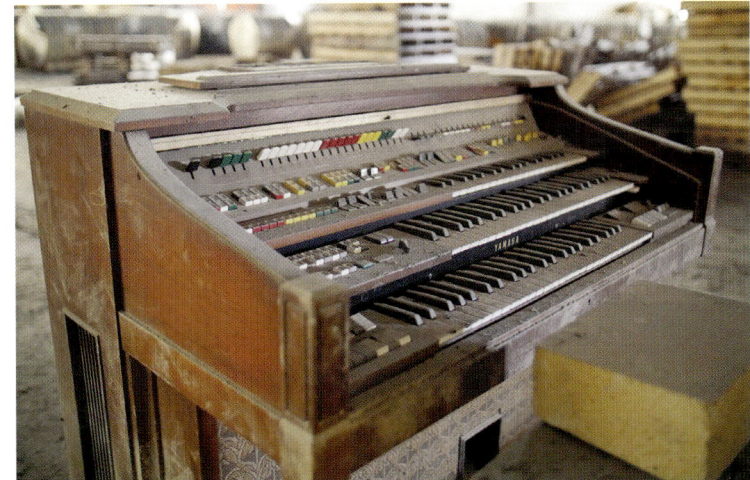

Something that one would not normally expect to find at a disused cement works!

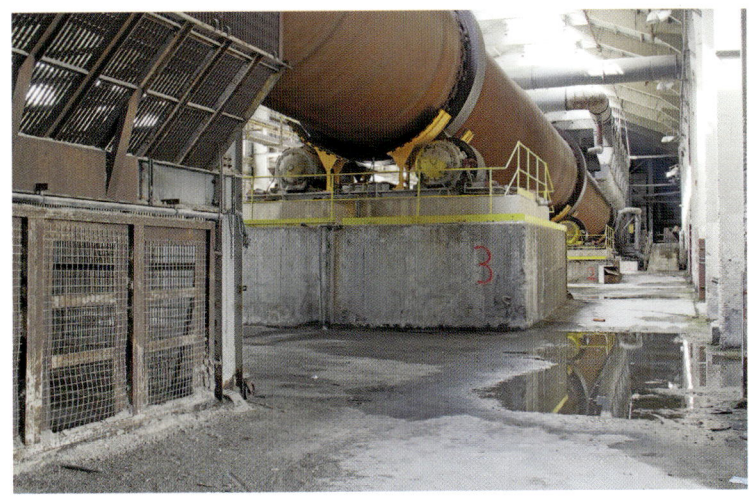

Kiln No. 2, looking towards the hot end.

Westbury Cement Works: An Illustrated History

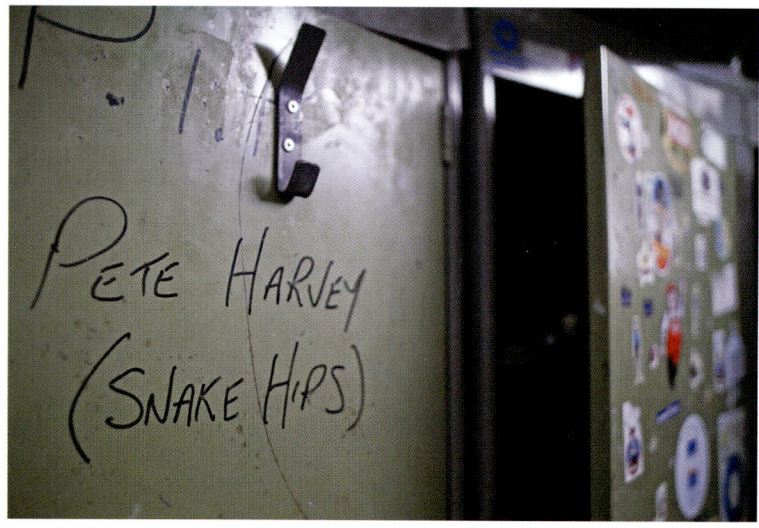

The locker rooms.

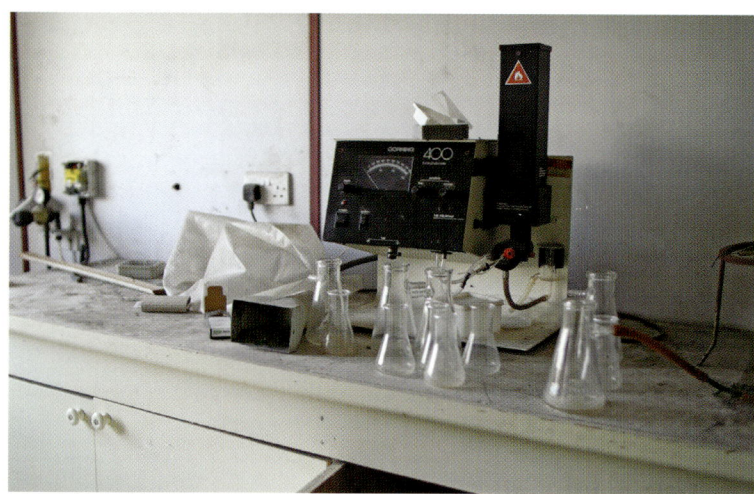

Equipment left in the laboratory.

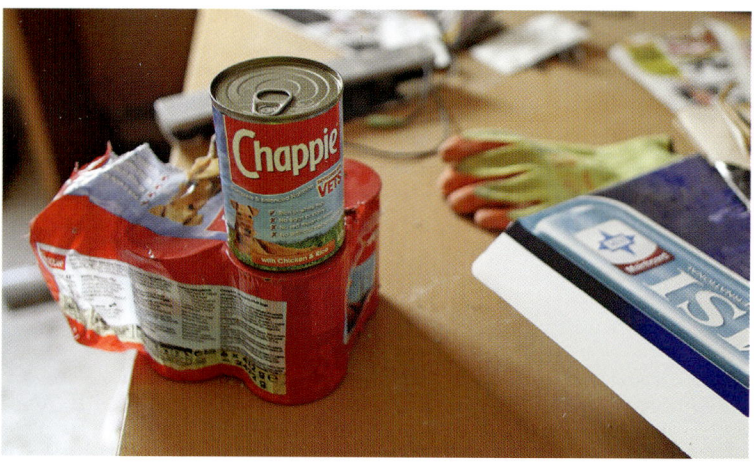

Food for the security dogs that was also used to feed the local foxes.

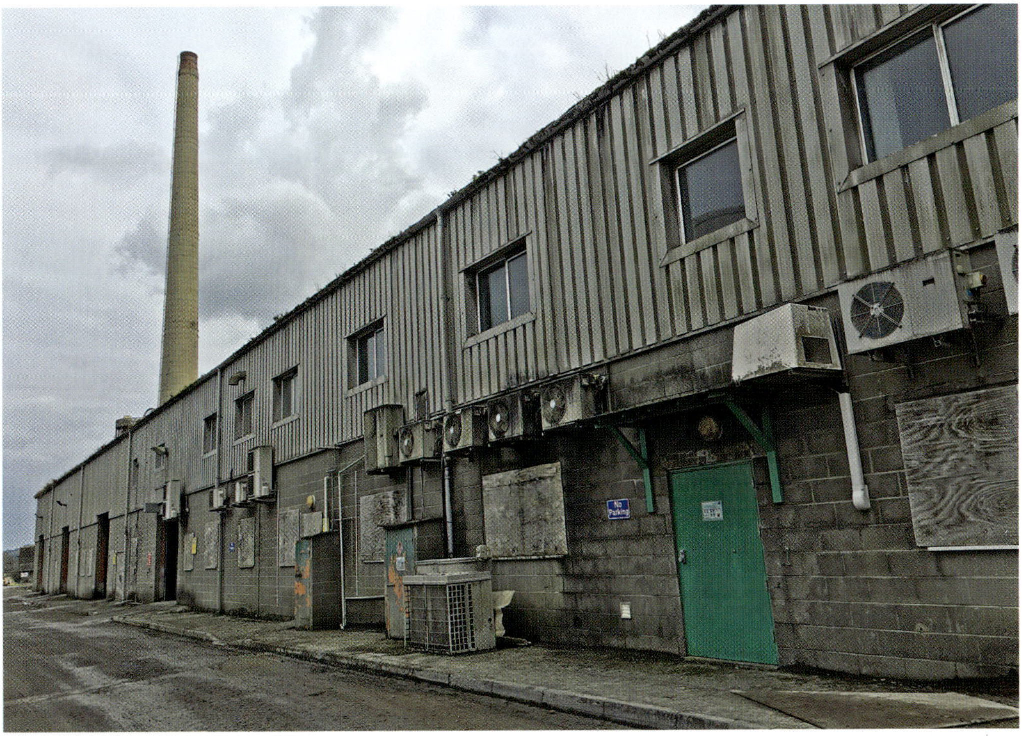

A Ghost Town

The workshops.

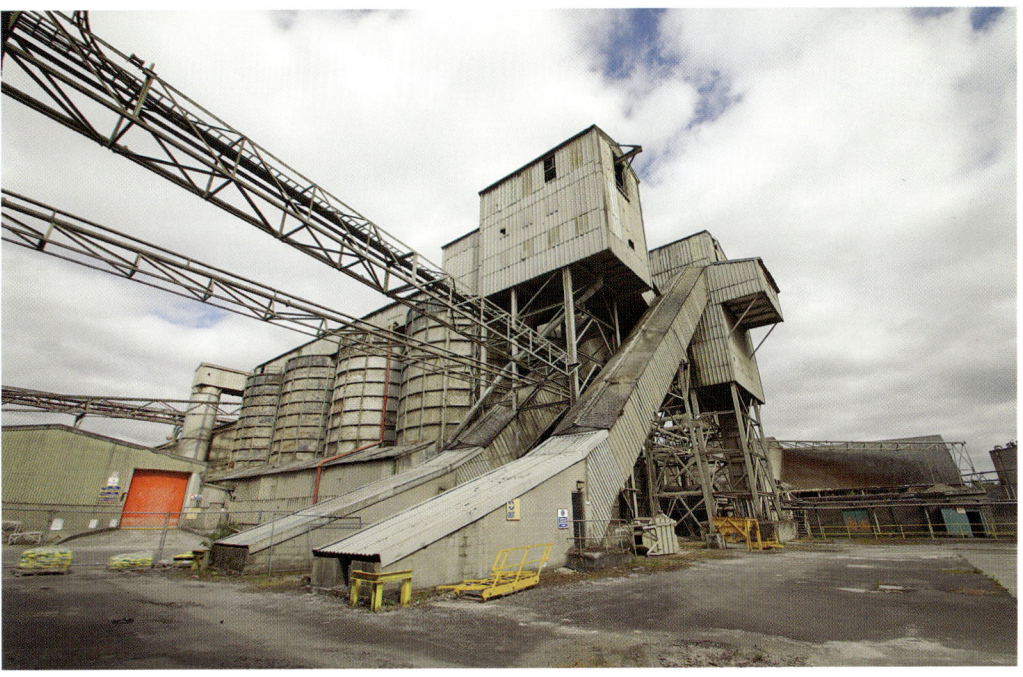

The clinker conveyor. (Copyright Nigel Osman)

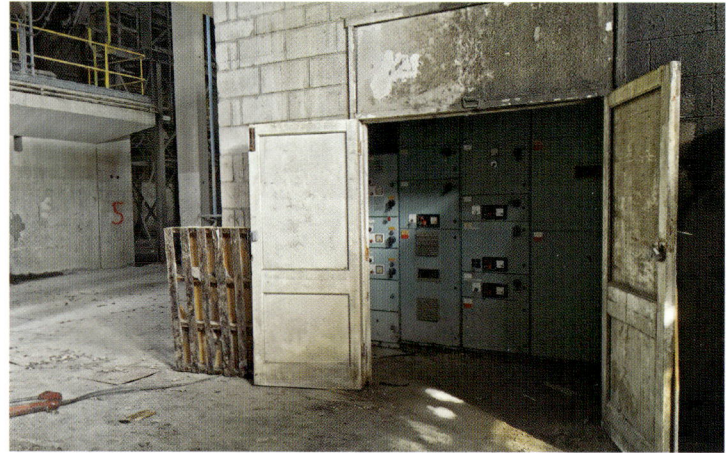

The electrical switch room that controlled the dust return to the kiln.

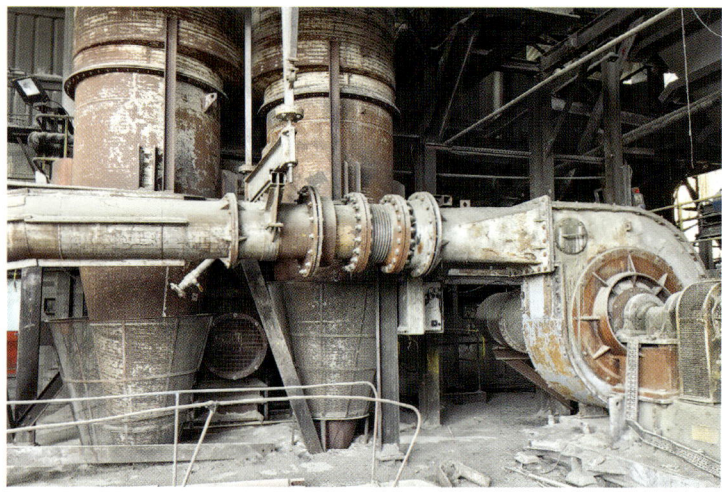

The firing fan that blew the coal into the kiln.

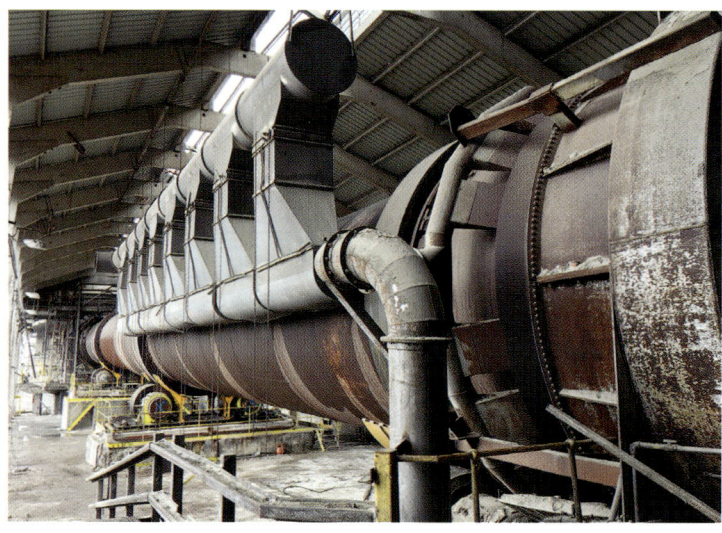

The burning zone end of the kiln where the kiln shell was cooled.

Chapter 7

Hidden Wildlife

As previously mentioned, when I first set foot on the site in February 2016, the only moment that really stirred any excitement was getting my first sight of the peregrine falcons as they perched on the chimney. Before this I had only ever had a fleeting glimpse of a peregrine as it sped past me on the Dorset coast, so to be able to spend the best part of a day watching a pair of them was a privilege. Little did I know during this first visit on that cold Saturday in February that the site's wildlife would come to truly captivate me.

Naturally, with the peregrines being my only highlight from that first visit, they grabbed my attention the most as far as the work's wildlife was concerned, and in 2015, the first time the peregrines nested on site, two eggs were laid on the clinker storage silos. Both hatched, but only one chick survived to successfully fledge.

In the hope that the birds would once again nest on the clinker silos, in 2016 Nigel worked with Roger Martindale (the site's ecologist) to cut a small hole in the wall of the gypsum storage conveyor building, which would then allow them to monitor the birds and any of the prospective illegal activities that such birds can attract. The hole was just big enough to fit a camera lens through or view the nest with binoculars. This meant that all viewing of the birds would be from inside a building and would not cause a disturbance to them. The hole, one of many that was cut in case the birds chose another location to nest, was cut right at the beginning of the year, long before the birds had chosen a nest site. It would mean that if they did nest within line of sight of one of the holes in the wall, Roger and Nigel could easily monitor the birds' progress and check the security of the nest site. This was especially important as Roger needed to know if the demolition of the site would affect the birds in any way. It also meant that there would now be an anxious wait of around four months until anyone knew if the conveyor building would serve one last and very important purpose as a hide, before its demolition. It was therefore met with much excitement and relief when the female peregrine eventually chose to once again nest on the clinker silos.

Choosing to nest on a demolition site might not seem like a good idea, but in 2016 the peregrines chose their nesting site very well – even better than the previous year. Years ago, an old electrical cabinet had been put outside, on top of the clinker silos. The bottom panel of the cabinet was missing, and this proved to make the perfect nest as the eggs were laid inside the cabinet, which provided shelter from the wind and rain. It was high up, around 80 feet, which, although not as high as say, Salisbury Cathedral, where peregrines also nest, proved to be high enough for this family. Three eggs were laid from 6 to 13 April, with the chicks hatching on 15 and 16 May.

At the time of nesting, the demolition was due to continue around the gypsum silos, but this was no longer possible once the silos had been chosen as the nest site. To avoid disturbing the nesting birds, the demolition of the site was halted in the nest area and only continued well away from the birds. Even with the demolition happening well away from the nest, it was obviously still noisy for the birds during the day. The heavy machinery would often make the ground shake and vibrations could sometimes be felt throughout most of the site. But this did not seem to bother the peregrines as they had become habituated to this level of noise and machinery movements, which had been carefully assessed as not being a threat to them breeding.

During the nesting period the parent birds continued to provide for their fast-growing family, bringing to the nest many different species of prey for their young. Sometimes, as the heavy machinery slowly rumbled along the road below the nest, the three chicks would peer curiously over the edge. I would wonder what was going through their young minds, what were they thinking of these strange, yellow, monstrous machines. However, as soon as a meal was delivered by mum or dad, all interest in the outside world was lost as the three young birds were being fed.

The youngsters were getting their first insights into human activity – on a demolition site of all places. For the first six weeks of their lives they had only experienced an 80-foot-high, northerly view of the world, but because Tarmac and Cuddy made the effort to cooperate and live side by side with nature, the three peregrine chicks would get a chance to experience the world from whatever viewpoint they chose.

I was extremely fortunate to be able to make a few visits to view the nest, and it was quite a trek to get there. The journey started off in the clinker shed, following the belt that once delivered the clinker down from the silos. This progressed up a steep incline, you then made a 90-degree right turn, continued on an incline and levelled off where the belt was now over the mill house, at which point you would be around 80 feet above the ground. Once you'd walked the width of the mill house, you had to make a 180-degree left turn to double back over the mill house. I would always stop at this point, often to catch my breath, but also to view the site and the chimney through a large, rectangular hole that had been cut in the wall there. I would also take the opportunity to remove my hard hat and high visibility top, so that I wasn't presenting a bright colour as I walked past the small viewing hole in the wall. The last leg was to continue along to the end of the narrow passage way, heading back towards the clinker shed. In the heat of the summer it was a hot slog in my PPE gear, but it was always worth it. Once I had quietly set up my camera on the tripod and attached my separate viewing screen, I would then spend the next hour or so sat down, watching the screen, waiting for some action. This set-up meant that I would never see the parents arrive at the nest with my own eyes, but it also meant that there would be minimal movement from inside the building.

While the chicks were young, they spent most of their time sat down in the nest, patiently waiting for food to arrive. The moment one of the parent birds did arrive, the chicks would wake up, calling and straining their necks, as mum or dad pulled apart the latest meal and fed each of their offspring. When the parent left, silence returned to the nest. All three youngsters grew fast, with mum and dad proving to be great parents.

Hidden Wildlife

As they grew, they became more vocal and active. Feathers replaced the soft, white fluffy down and they soon started stretching their wings. The stretching then turned to flapping as their flight instinct began to kick in and they would stand on the very edge of the silo, exercising those all-important flight muscles.

I had to pinch myself the first time I saw the birds on the nest. I was on a demolition site, the air was filled with noise, and sometimes the ground would shake, but these magnificent creatures seemed almost oblivious to what was going on around them. To the three chicks, until they left the nest, all of this would have been normal to them. As far as they were concerned, this was what the world was like. This was the last place that I would expect this once heavily persecuted species to thrive. But thrive they did.

The parents would spend a lot of time perched on the chimney, often being very vocal while they were there. It was a favourite perch for the birds, giving them the perfect location to survey their domain. If the parents weren't out hunting or on the nest, chances were they would be perched on the ladder of the chimney.

The twelve-week period of cooperation between man and nature proved every bit worthwhile. It only takes some effort and consideration for us to live side by side with nature, and with careful observation Tarmac and Cuddy, under the guidance of Nigel and Roger, ensured the safety of the peregrines during the nesting season and all three chicks had fledged by 24 June.

The young birds could be seen hanging around the site in the following weeks after fledging, with the parent birds continuing to provide food and teaching them all the vital skills required to go on to become successful hunters themselves. One afternoon I watched in awe as a dog fight played out over the site between a young peregrine and, on this occasion, one very lucky pigeon. The chase only lasted a few seconds before the pigeon was able to twist and turn to outmanoeuvre the peregrine. This was natural selection playing out before my eyes.

It was truly a privilege to have been able to observe such a stunning animal grow from a shaky fragile chick to one of nature's fastest and most efficient aerial hunting machines.

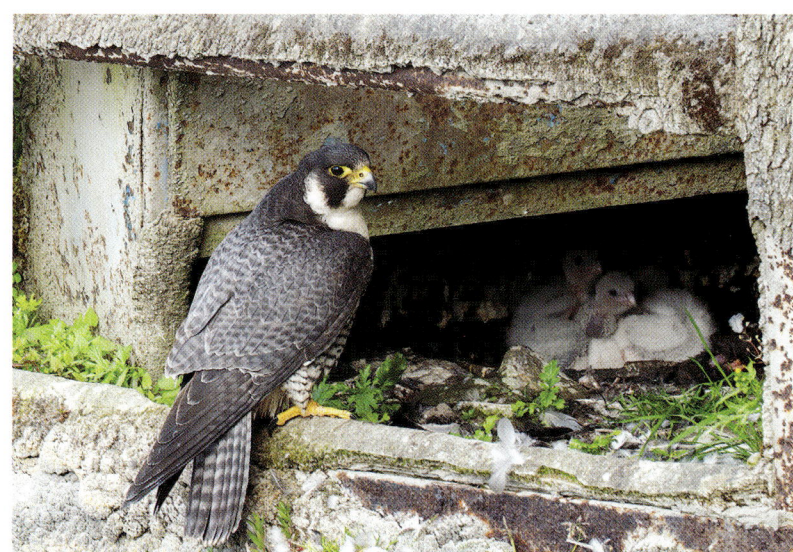

The male peregrine (*Falco peregrinus*) returns to the nest to feed the chicks.

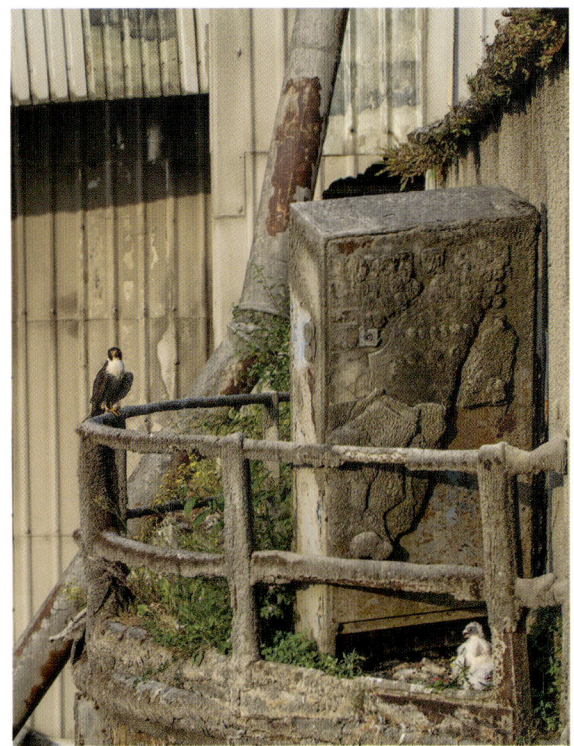

Left: A hot June evening and mum perches on the silo railing, wings open to help keep cool. The old electrical cabinet serves as a perfect nest.

Below: Mum keeping a watchful eye on the nest below.

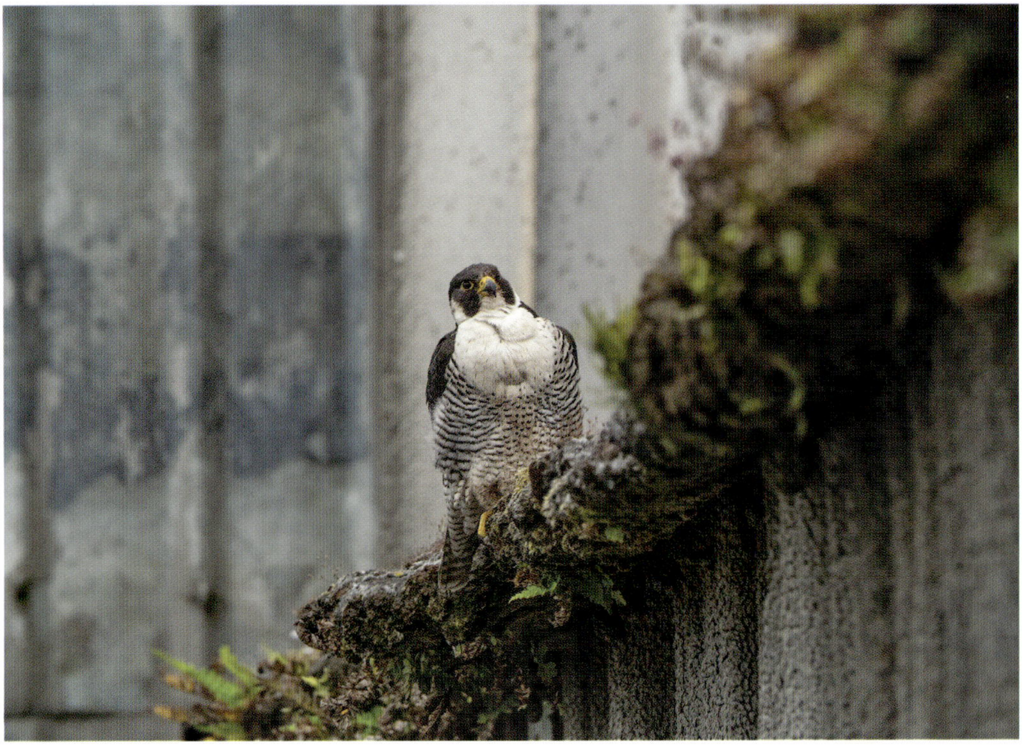

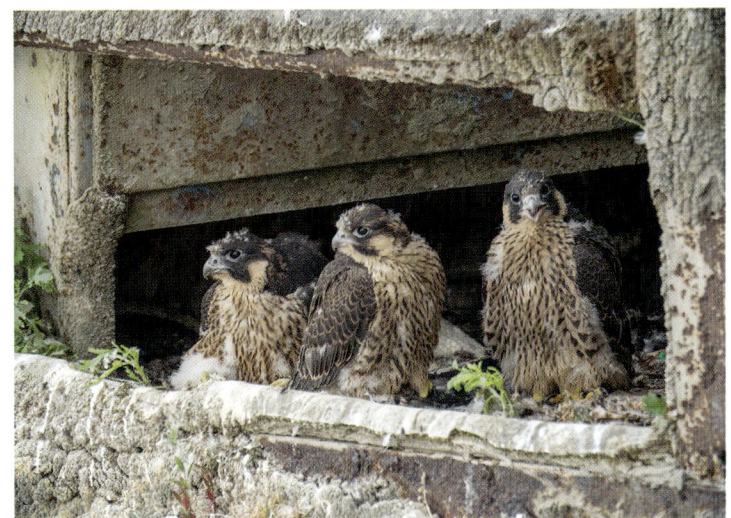

Three fast-growing youngsters, with not many down feathers left to shed.

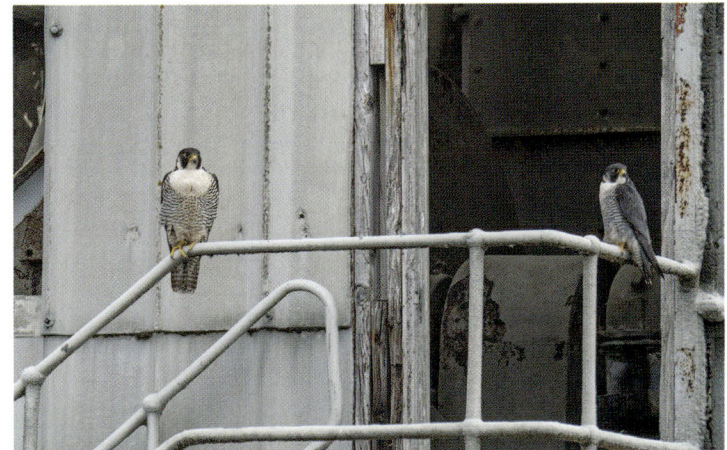

Both mum (on the left) and dad keeping a watchful eye on the nest from the clinker return elevator.

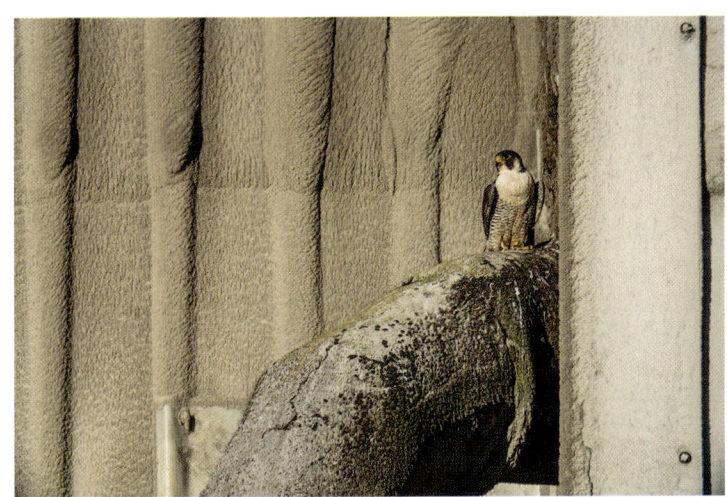

Another favourite perch – the dust extraction pipe from the clinker handling building.

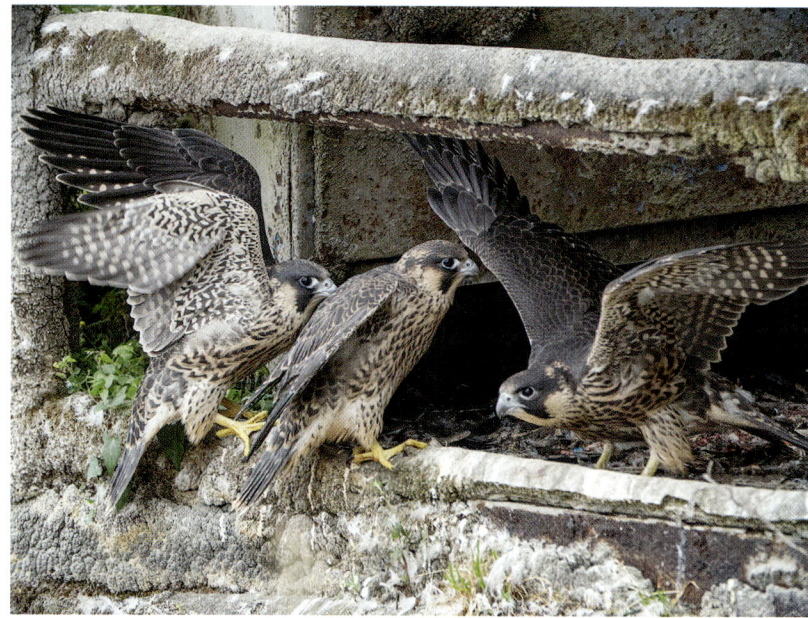

With their flight feathers now fully formed, a great deal of wing stretching and flapping takes place. More time is spent on the very edge of the nest now as an eagerness to take to the air starts to overwhelm the youngsters.

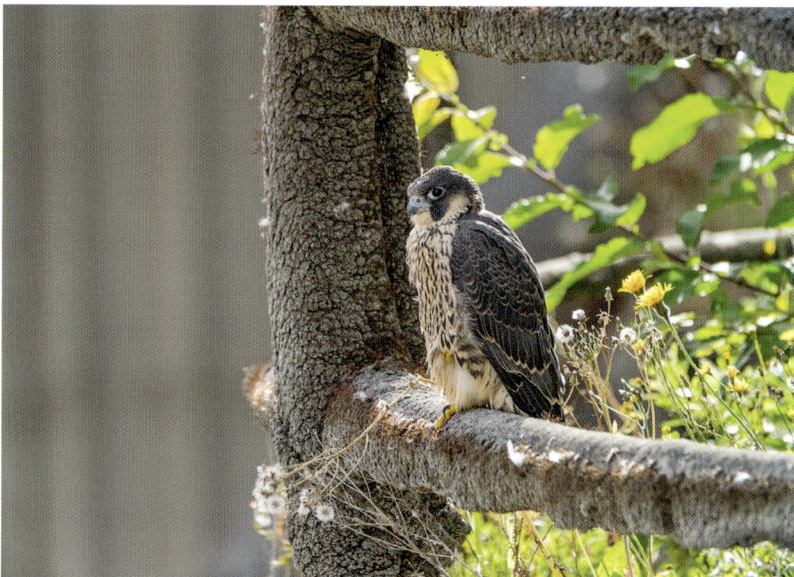

Hanging around the nest after a successful first flight.

 As well as the peregrines, the site hosts many other species of flora and fauna. The reed beds around the ponds provide the perfect habitat for reed warblers and reed buntings. The insect life around and in the ponds, as well as feeding the warblers and buntings, also provides plenty of food for swallows, swifts and house martins. Ducks, swans, moorhens, coots, canada geese and herons also make homes on the ponds and clay quarry lake.

 The clay stock pile on site has become its own habitat now. In summer and through to early autumn it is awash with common ragwort. This swaying sea of yellow flowers

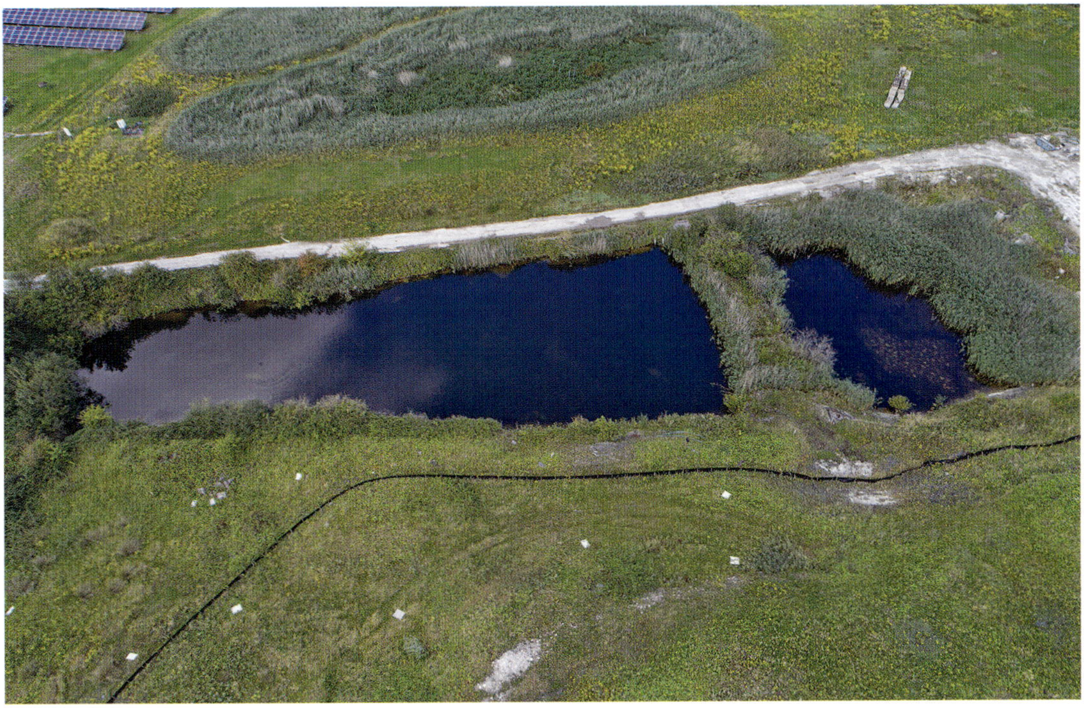

Hidden Wildlife

The ponds on the north edge of the works. The white squares on the ground are metal sheets, used to attract reptiles.

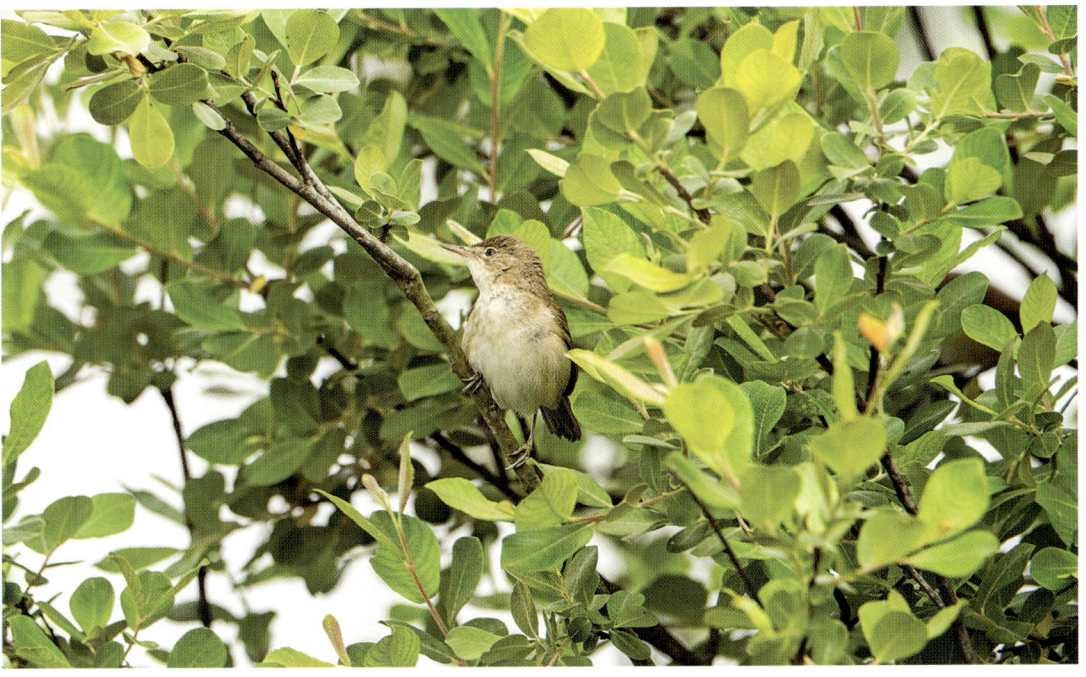

Reed warbler (*Acrocephalus scirpaceus*).

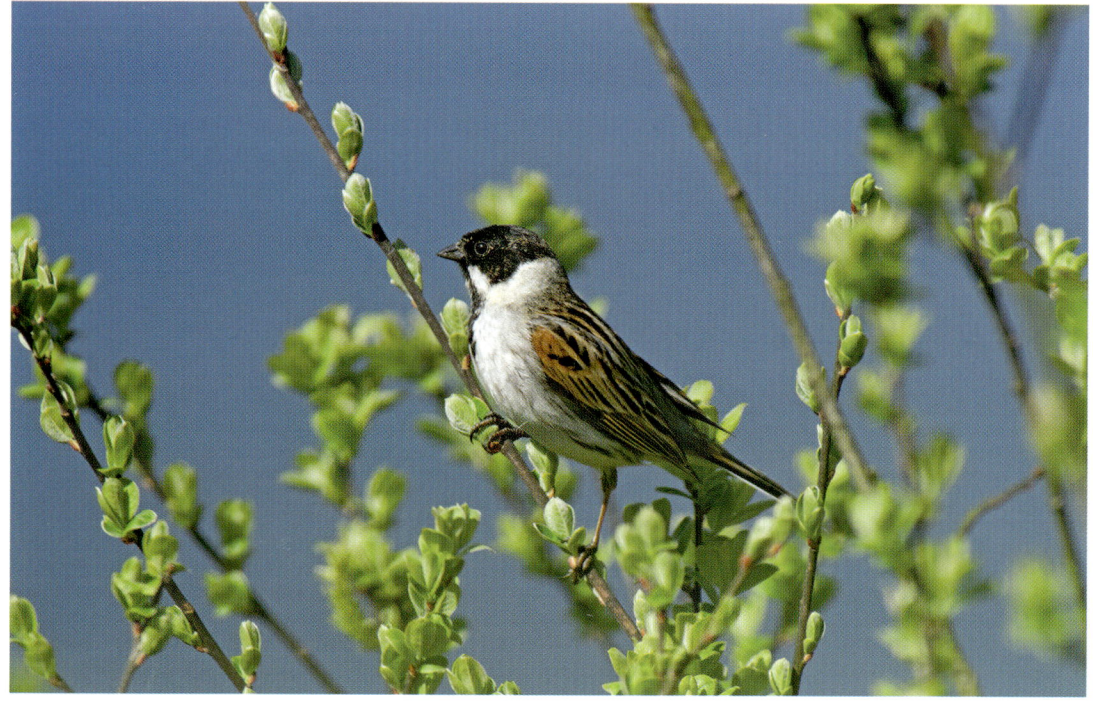

Reed bunting (*Emberiza schoeniclus*). (Copyright Nigel Osman)

attracts bees, moths and butterflies. As the bees go about their daily routine of collecting pollen, the tiny but beautiful common blue butterfly also frequents the area. Small numbers of clouded yellow butterflies can also be seen in the area. This fast-flying migrant species is almost impossible to spot among the yellow ragwort. It is only when it has taken to the air that its distinctive orange-yellow wings catch the eye.

Below the canopy of yellow, field voles take sanctuary. The area provides the little mammal with its diet of grass and roots, and because in nature there is usually something bigger to prey on something smaller, the voles are a good food source for the kestrels that can often be seen hunting over the clay stock pile. The voles can often be found under metal sheets that Nigel has placed around the area. The sheets were put out to offer warm places for reptiles – the slow-worms, grass snakes and lizards – but the voles also discovered that they provide a nice place to take shelter. I'm sure that the voles also know that the kestrel can't get to them while they are under the sheets!

Occasionally, one or two brown hares can be seen on site and they also seem to like the clay stock pile. They feed on the grass that grows among the ragwort and thistles and, strangely, they seem to have been quite relaxed on the odd occasion that I have inadvertently stumbled upon them.

When the ground softens after rain, the exposed clay often shows signs that badgers, deer and foxes have been exploring during the night, with numerous footprints and tracks left behind. The badger prints are from the family members that are residents of the extensive sett that borders the east edge of the site. To observe these larger mammals, camera traps were set up around the site and they helped confirm what the footprints were telling us, as the following images show.

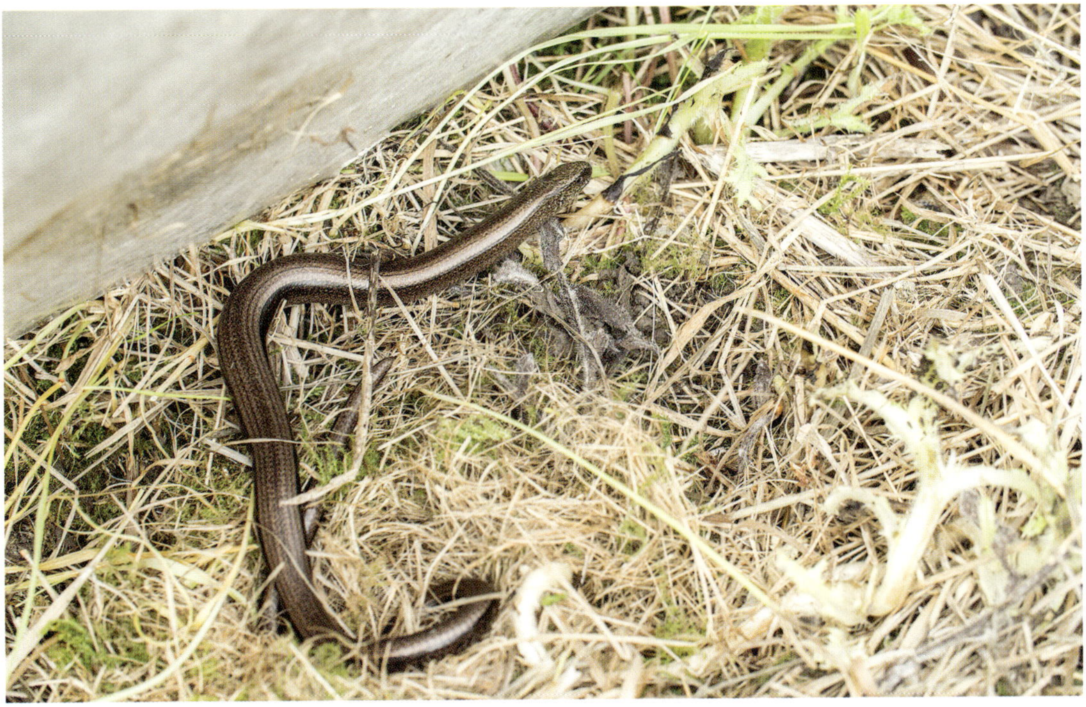

Slow-worm (*Anguis fragilis*).

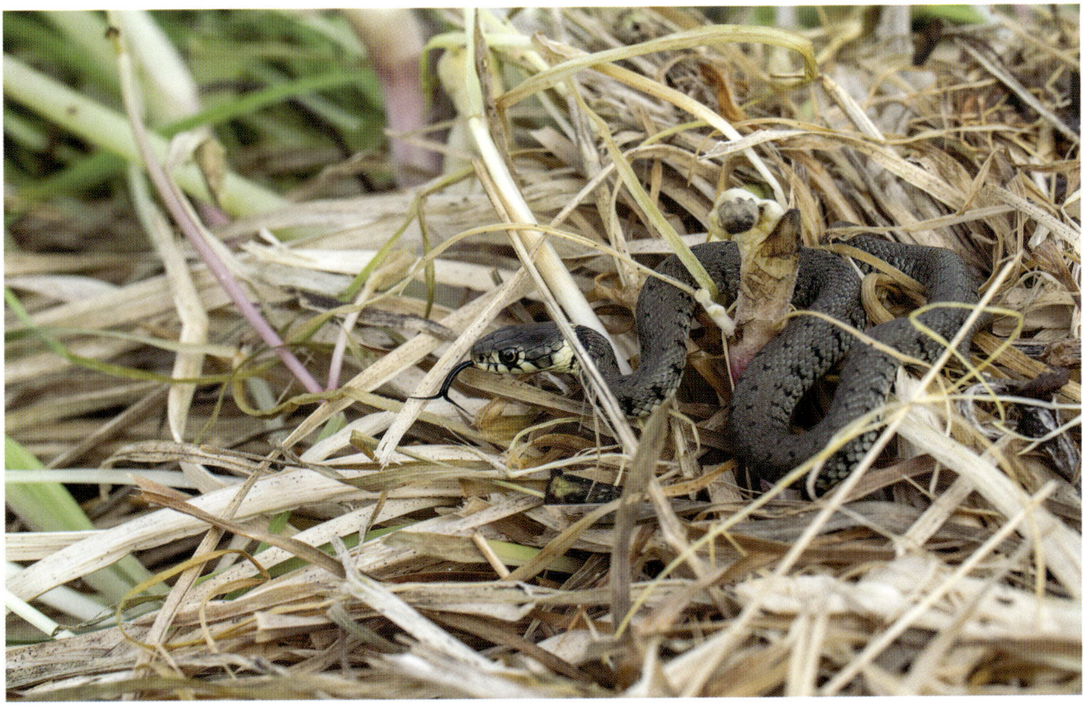

Grass snake (*Natrix natrix*). This young snake is barely thicker than a pencil.

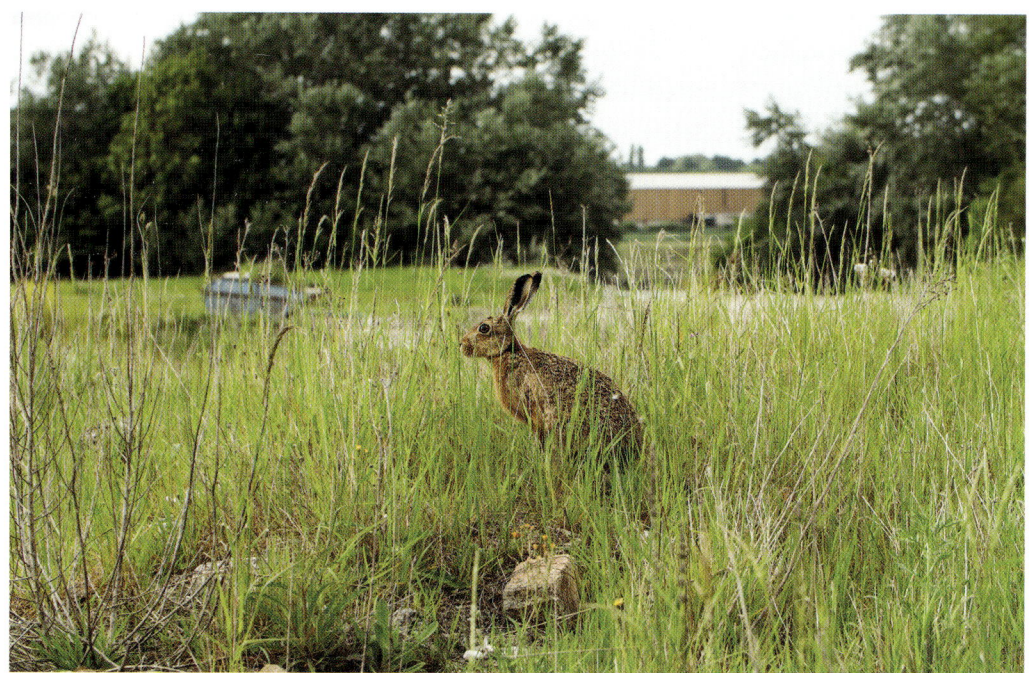

Brown hare (*Lepus europaeus*).

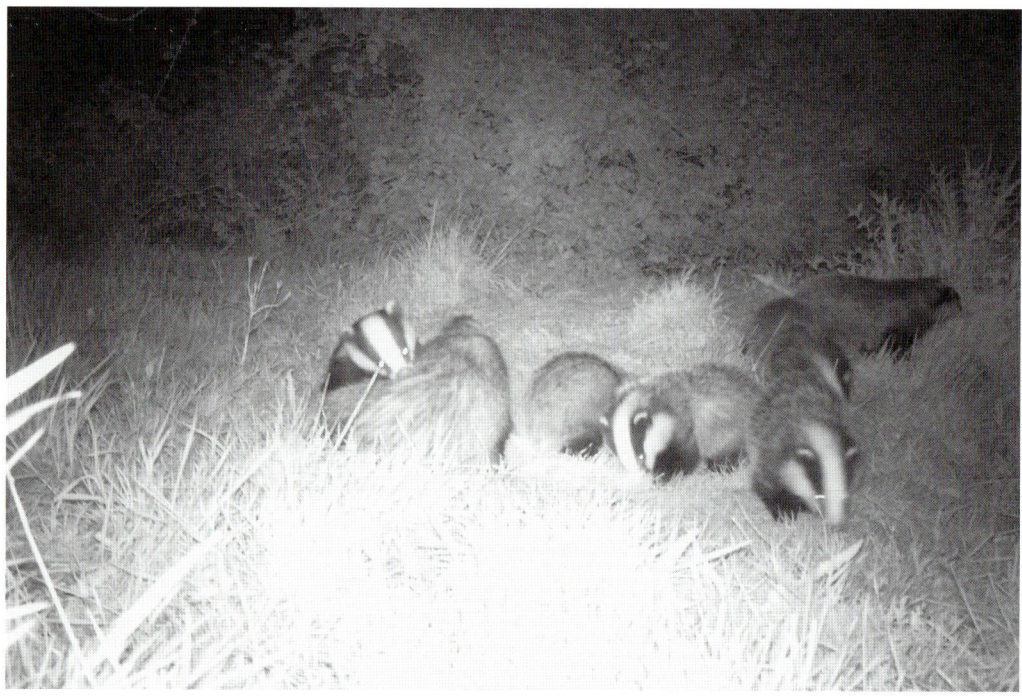

Badger (*Meles meles*). Taken at 4.42 a.m., this image shows seven of the works' social group foraging for food and grooming each other. (Copyright Nigel Osman)

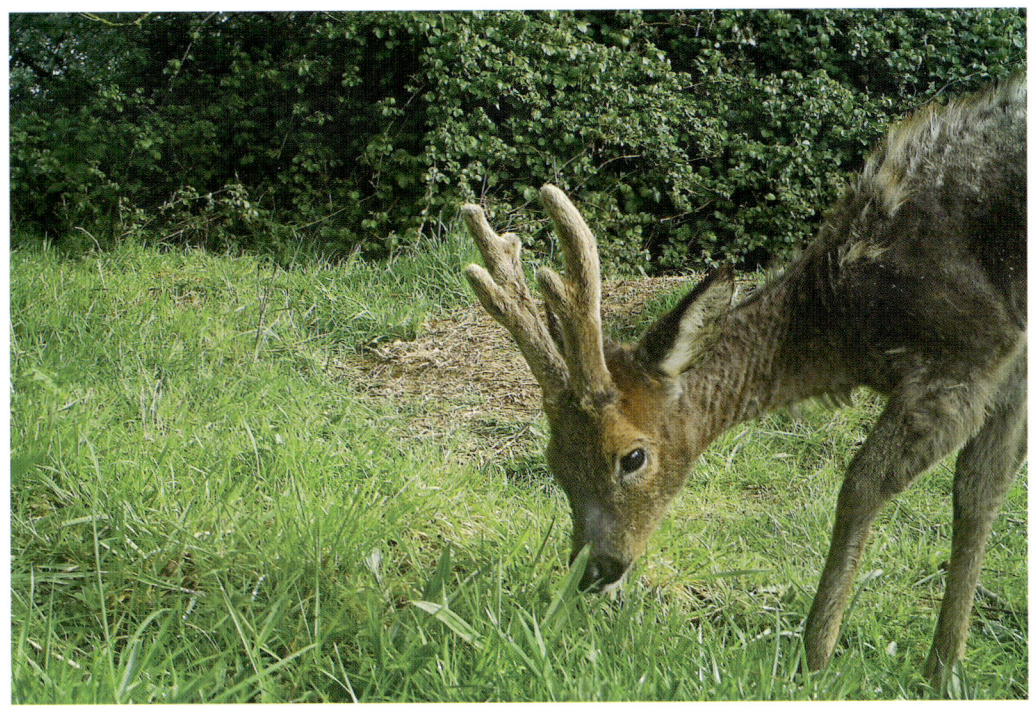

Roe deer (*Capreolus carpreolus*). (Copyright Nigel Osman)

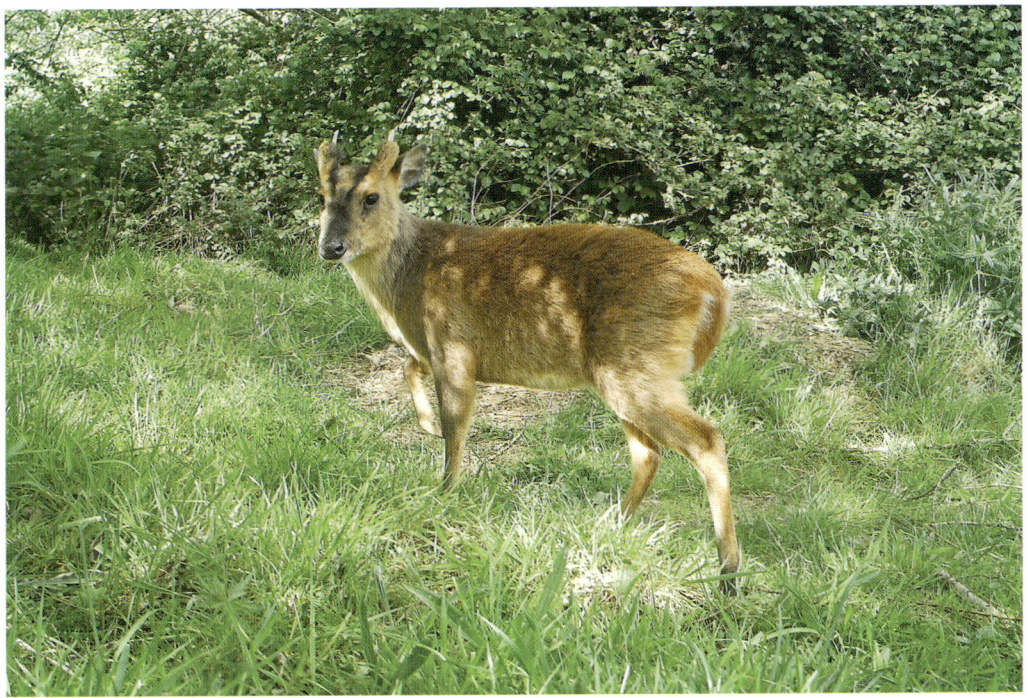

Muntjac (*Muntiacus reevesi*). (Copyright Nigel Osman)

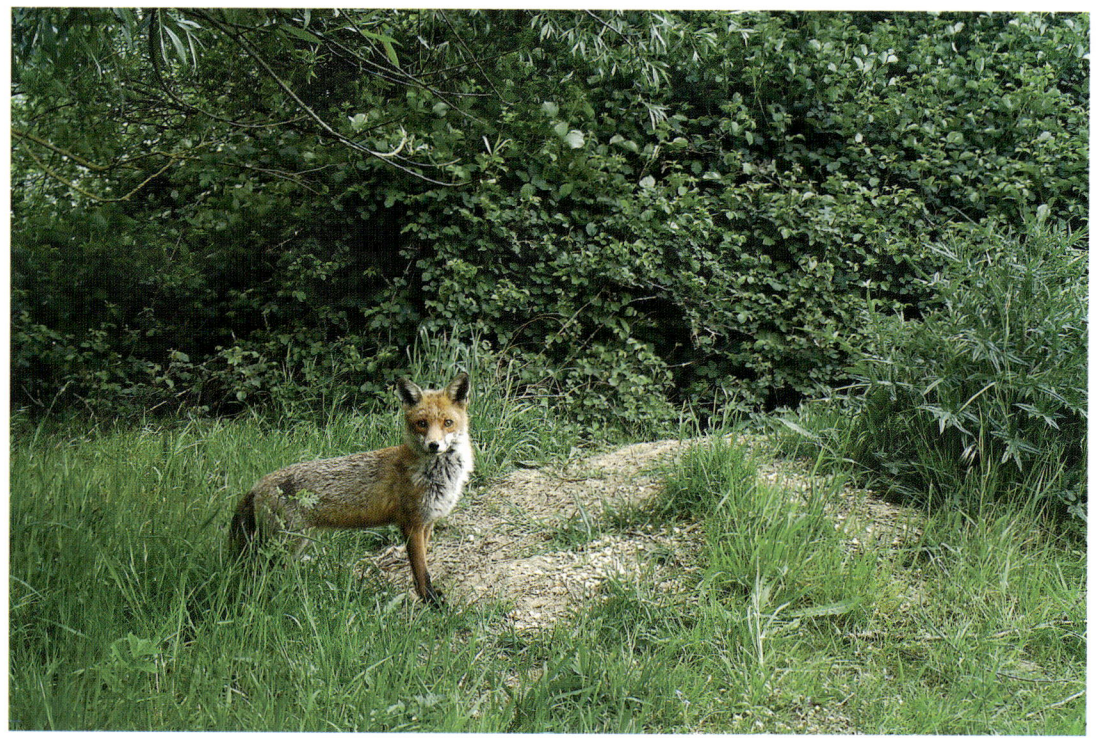

Red fox (*Vulpes vulpes*). (Copyright Nigel Osman)

As much as the clay pile has now become its own small ecosystem, the area of the storage ponds now feels like a miniature nature reserve. Standing in between the first pond and the bank where the chimney came to rest, and with the silence that now blankets the site, it is easy to forget where you are. From this location, the tops of the cement silos are the only indication you get as to where you are. Here, on warm summer days, blue tits dart out from the trees to catch insects on the wing, as reed warblers sing from the brambles. The ponds themselves provide good hunting grounds for kingfishers. Often the sharp, unmistakable *'cheee, cheee'* call will alert you to their presence before you spot them. They spend their time working the banks, using the overhanging willow trees, bushes and dead branches that protrude from the water's edge to ambush the stickleback that populate the ponds. The huge variety of aquatic insect life in the area also helps to supplement this stunning bird's diet throughout the summer months. Camera traps and a homemade perch were used to get some close-up pictures of what we had only been able to observe from a distance.

The storage ponds were once heavily populated with carp. In fact, the carp from the cooling ponds were originally used to stock the fishing lake in the Country Park. Sadly, now the ponds show hardly any signs that anything bigger than stickleback populate these waters. Signs of otters have been observed in the stream that runs on the edge of the site, so it would be a reasonable assumption that otters have led to the demise of the carp. Cormorant are sometimes present on the ponds, as are grey herons. These fish-eating birds could also be partly responsible for the loss of the once prevalent species.

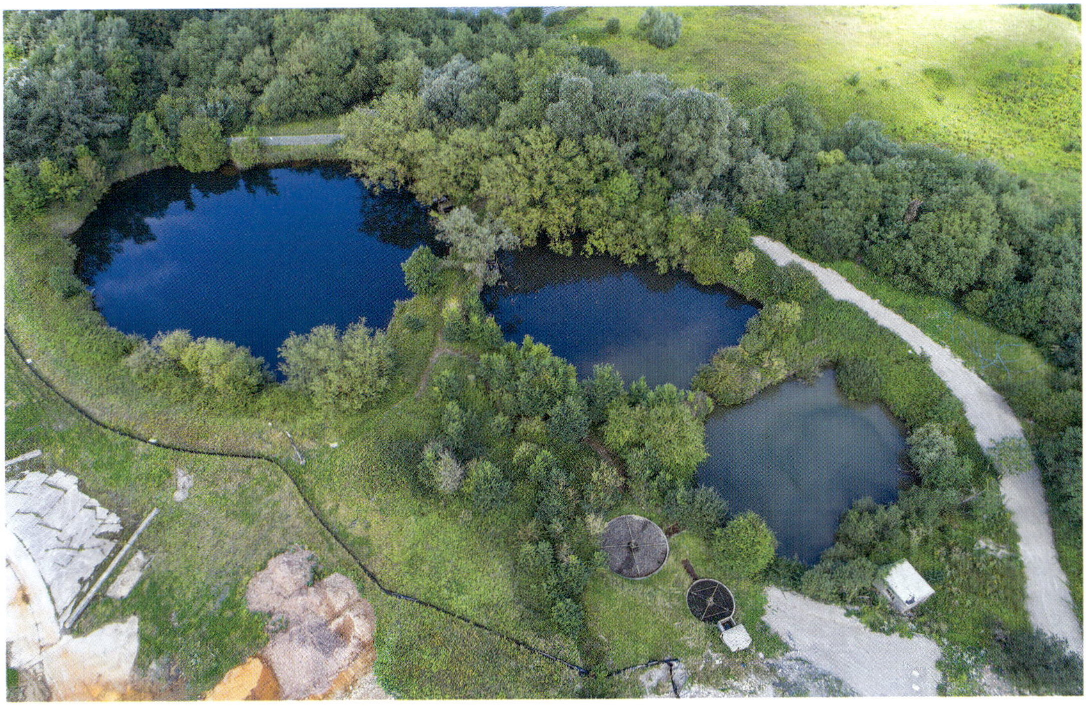

Hidden Wildlife

The storage ponds helped to fulfil any extra water requirements that the works may have had.

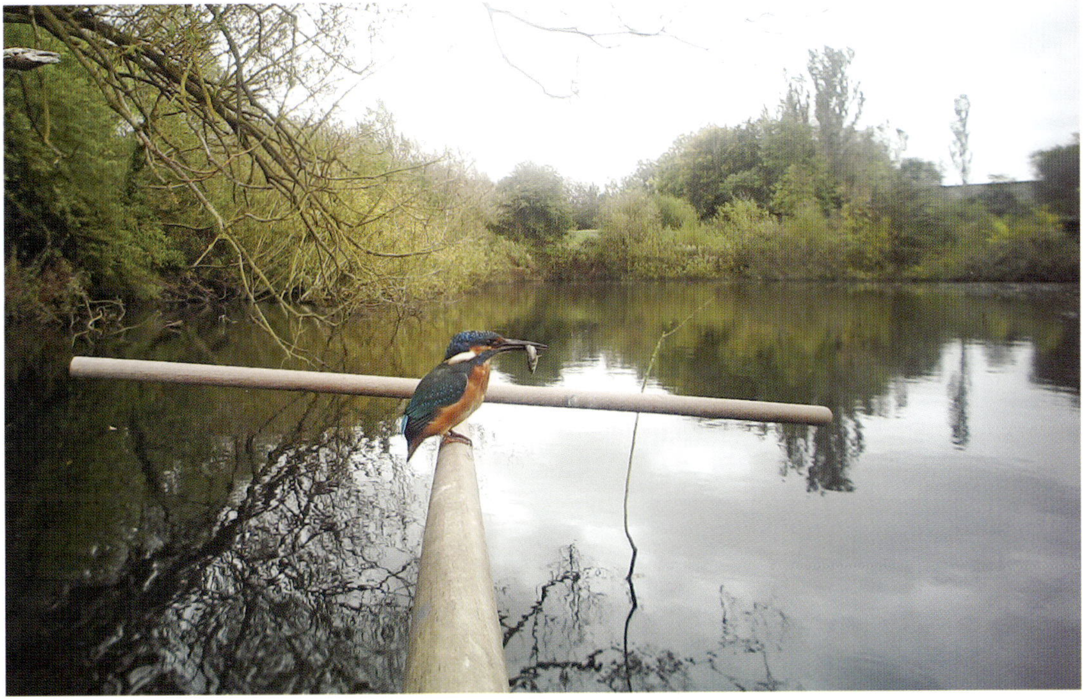

Kingfisher (*Alcedo atthis*) with a stickleback. (Copyright Nigel Osman)

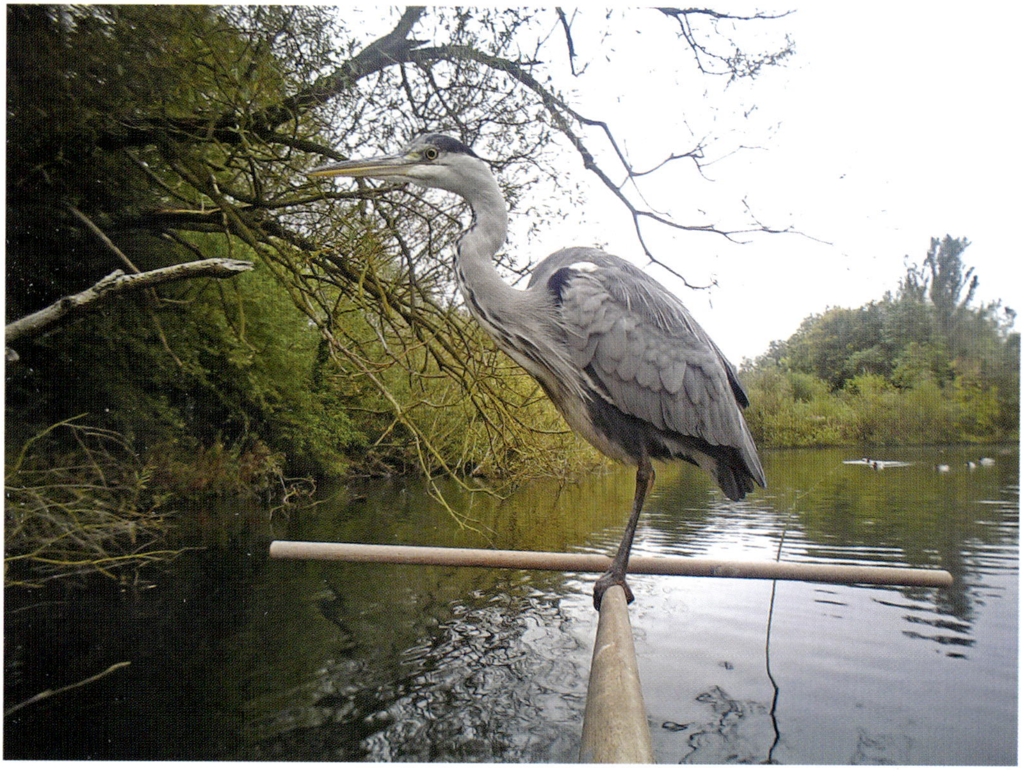

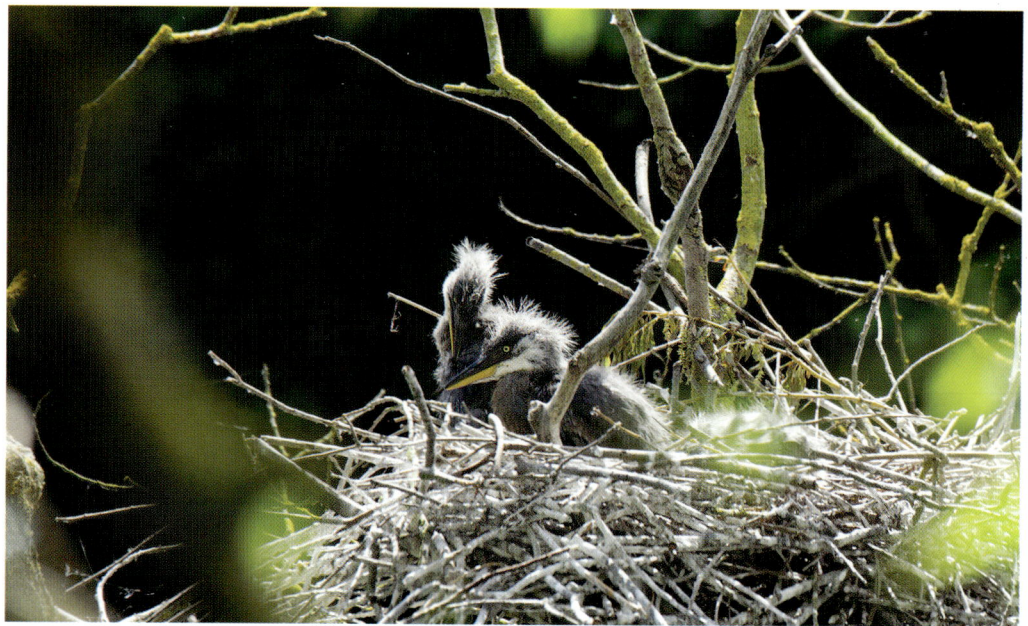

Grey heron (*Ardea cinerea*). (Copyright Nigel Osman)

Grey heron chicks on the nest in 2015. (Copyright Nigel Osman)

Hidden Wildlife

The area behind the clay quarry hosts good populations of common spotted and pyramidal orchids from June to August. The pink and cerise of the orchids stand prominent against the bright yellow of the bird's-foot trefoil and the white of the oxeye daisies, as damselflies gently drift through the vegetation. The abundance of wild flowers naturally makes this another great location for bees.

There are also bats. Lesser horseshoe and brown long-eared bats roost in some of the buildings that are left. Much to my surprise, one of the buildings they like is the sub-station. This surprises me because the huge transformer in the building produces a very loud buzzing sound. This doesn't seem to bother the bats though! The lesser horseshoes also like to roost in the small brick sewage treatment plant building. After the chimney came down Nigel re-fitted the door to the building and boarded up the window, making sure that there was a 'bat friendly' entrance in the boarded-up window. He also installed some heaters that keep the temperature up during winter. These modifications have turned it into a near perfect roost for the lesser horseshoes. Brown long-eared bats are sometimes found in the building on the edge of the site, next to the cooling ponds. Again, Nigel has modified this building to make it more bat friendly. Bat boxes have also been placed near the ponds. Given time, it is very likely that this population will grow, as with plenty of water nearby there will always be an abundance of the all-important insect life that the bats require.

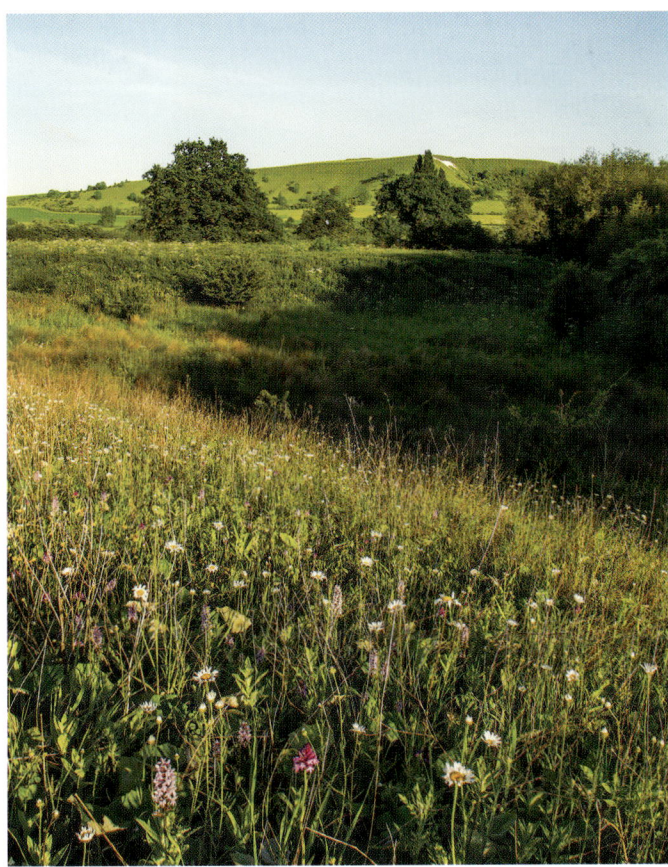

The view from behind the clay quarry, looking south toward the White Horse.

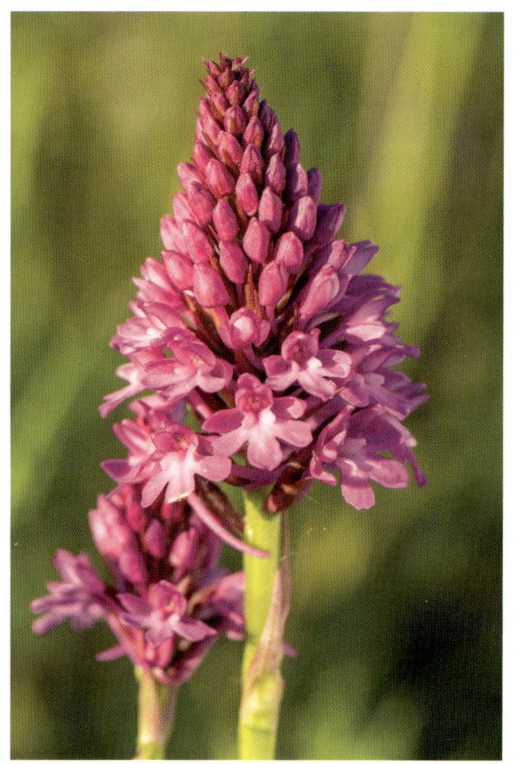 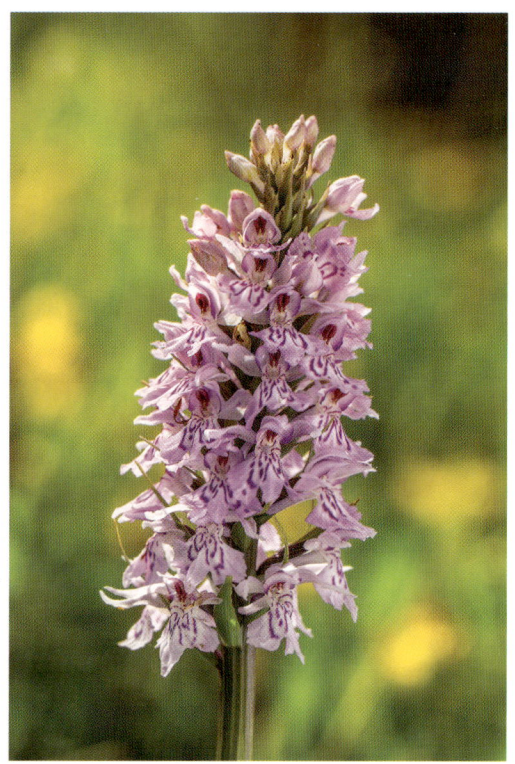

Above left: Pyramidal orchid (*Anacamptis pyramidalis*).

Above right: Common spotted orchid (*Dactylorhiza fuchsii*).

Below: Small tortoiseshell (*Nymphalis urticae*).

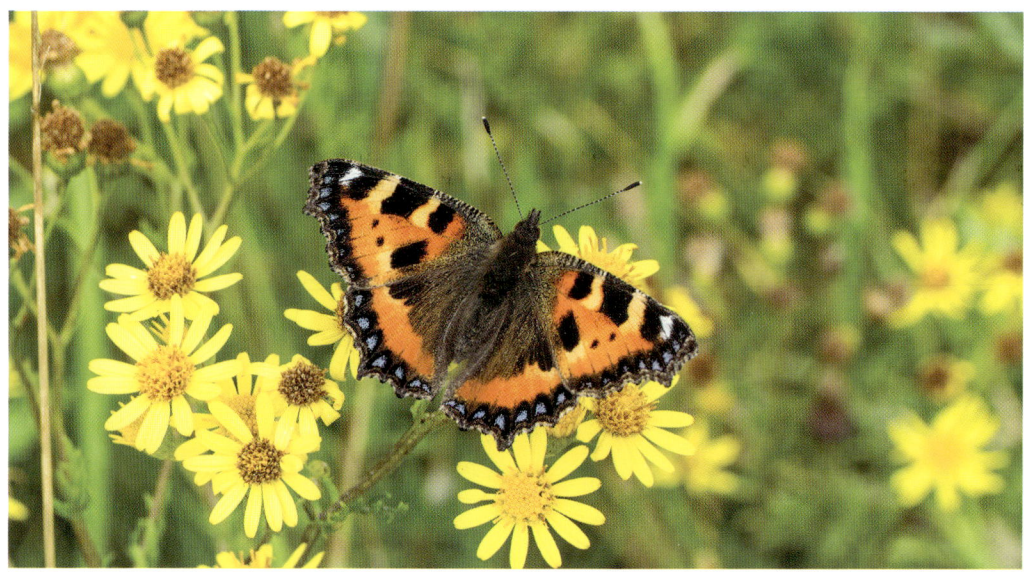

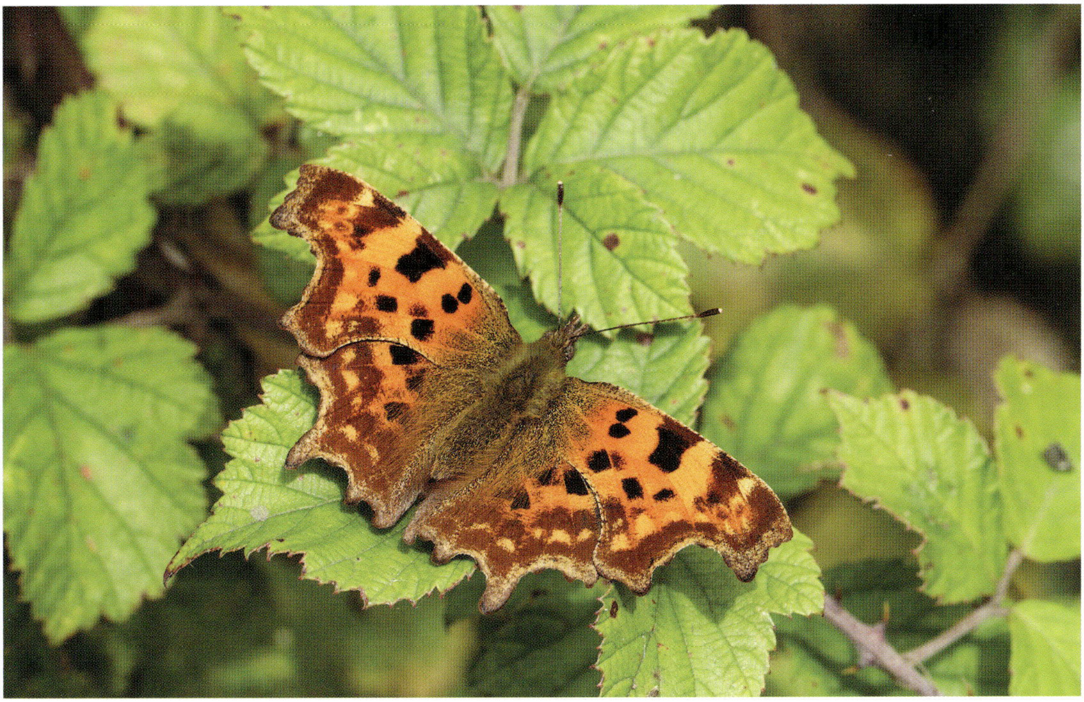

Hidden Wildlife

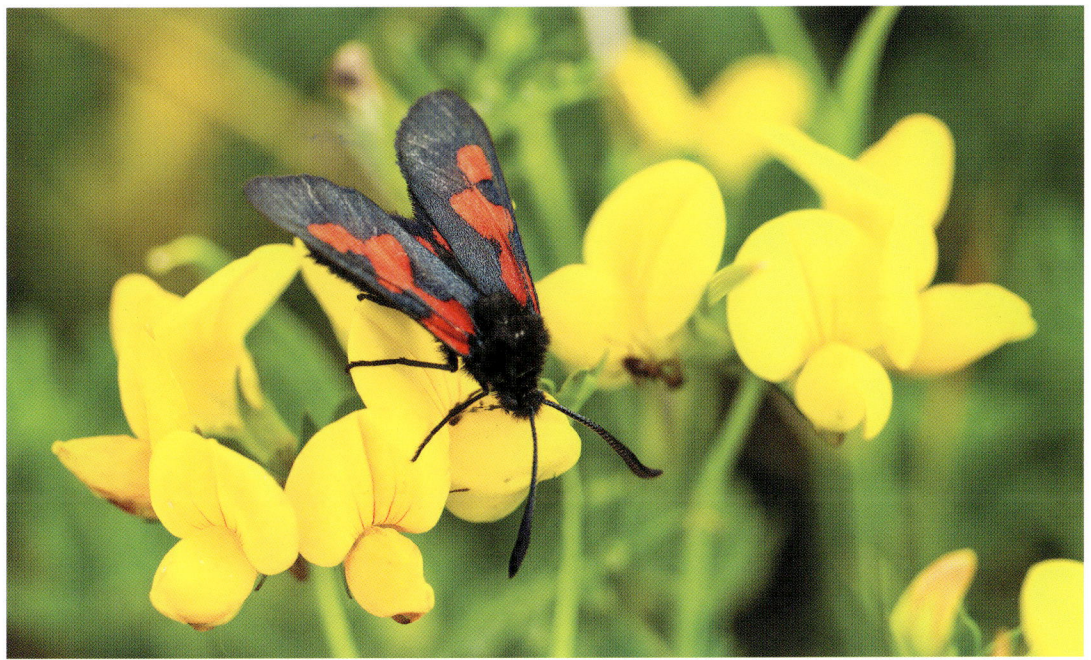

Comma (*Nymphalis c-album*).

Six-spot burnet (*Zygaena filipendulae*). Unusually, this specimen's three pairs of spots are fused together.

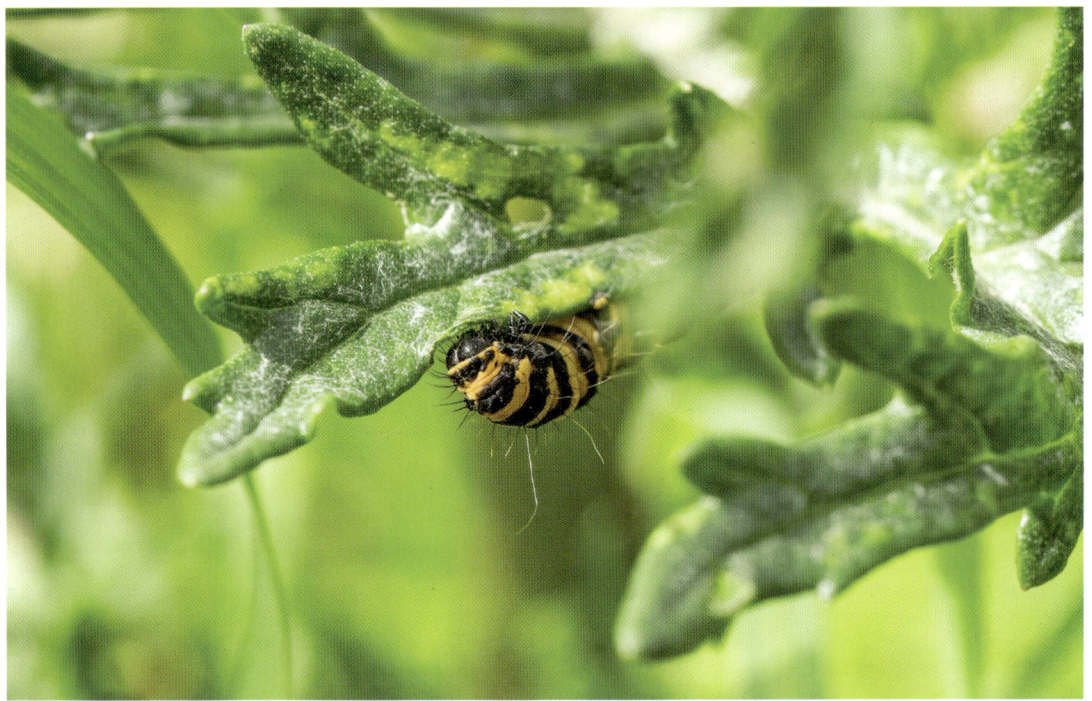

The cinnabar moth caterpillar (*Tyria jacobaeae*).

Returning to the sub-station, it proves once again that wildlife can adapt to its environment. Both a tawny owl and a barn owl have been caught on one of the site's many security cameras, visiting an owl nest box that Nigel has installed on one wall of the sub-station. As with the bats, the continuous buzz doesn't seem to bother them. With two species having been confirmed checking out the nest box, more boxes will be placed around the site to hopefully cater for multiple residents.

It is so peaceful and quiet on site now that when one is near the clay pile or ponds in summer, all that can be heard is birdsong, grasshoppers and bees. If you are very still and can find one, you can even hear the cinnabar caterpillar eating the succulent green leaves of the ragwort.

A once dusty and noisy site has now become a peaceful safe haven for some precious wildlife and this is mainly through the passion and hard work that Nigel has put into helping the works evolve through to the next chapter of its life.

Chapter 8

Deadly Doris

Long before the story of the cement industry would come to this small corner of Wiltshire and create its own history, there was another story waiting to be told that had been buried for aeons.

During the Jurassic Period, approximately 200 to 145 million years ago, the site was underwater. During this time, the mudstones that we now call the Kimmeridge Clay Formation were deposited as a sedimentary unit, stretching from Dorset to North Yorkshire in the UK. It was deposited in a marine environment, in warm and relatively shallow seas.

During this time when the Kimmeridge Clay was being deposited, dinosaurs ruled the land, pterosaurs were in the skies and the seas were populated with a plethora of marine life, with fish and marine reptiles dominating the waters. The latter included early crocodiles, ichthyosaurs, plesiosaurs and pliosaurs. The pliosaur was a huge carnivorous marine reptile. It would have been an apex predator in the Kimmeridgian seas and would have preyed upon fish, turtles and invertebrates called belemnites (a squid-like creature), and possibly even other marine retiles. It is with the pliosaur that this unique piece of the cement works history begins.

Around 150 million years ago one such pliosaur came to rest upon the sea floor during the continued deposition of the Kimmeridge Clay. Fortunately, the carcass would survive predation and any strong currents that could have disarticulated it, and time would bury it within the accumulating sediment and the process of preserving its remains as a fossil began.

Fast-forward to 1994, when the clay quarry was being excavated to provide the valuable raw materials required for the production of the cement, and amateur geologist Simon Carpenter could often be found looking for prehistoric remains in its grey sedimentary deposits. Simon regularly visited the quarry and was trusted by the works staff to be on site and collect any specimens that the machining of the quarry would sometimes reveal.

On 12 May 1994, when a new cycle of excavation had started, Simon was at the quarry in the evening, hoping that the new excavations would reveal some interesting specimens. High up in the corner of the quarry, close to its hedged boundary, he noticed a line of bone fragments that looked promising. As finding complete or partial skeletons is generally rare, and finding all of these bones together in the corner of the quarry, Simon knew that this could potentially be a significant find. But knowing how much of a significant find this was would take the hard work and dedication of Simon and a whole team of people. Simon recalls an evening that he will never forget and the exciting days that followed:

> I found the pliosaur at the end of an evening's reconnaissance of a new pit at the Westbury site. My visit coincided with a period of active quarrying, with a large quantity of clay having already been removed from the pit. The newly worked clays were dark and moist and studded with the nacreous and iridescent shells of ammonites and bivalves. On this particular occasion, I had traversed a slope on the far northeast side of the pit. This area had been graded back that very day to form a stable rim to the excavation. The first indications of a buried skeleton came when I noticed a line of broken bones protruding from the weathered clay near the top of the pit. The size of the fragments suggested that they belong to a reptile of substantial size. This was a very exciting moment, in spite of the fact that some bones had obviously already been lost, and others shattered as the excavators had worked across the clay. The failing light prevented me from doing much other than rescuing the fragments of bone scattered across the clay by the excavators. My main concern was that the area be would be left undisturbed until I could make a return trip to secure it the following day.
>
> The following day I contacted the quarry manager, Mr David Beatty, to inform him of the discovery. After work, I drove from my home in Bristol to Westbury to resume the search. Using a spade and a pickaxe I was able to begin removing clay from above the layer of bones. The first recognisable bone was a femur (propodial) which had a number of smaller paddle bones (epipodials and tarsals) associated with it. At the end of the evening I erected a simple barrier around the site and began to plan a day time visit at the weekend.
>
> My next step was to contact Dorset collector, Steve Etches. His knowledge and expertise as a collector and preparer of Kimmeridgian fossils is, in my opinion, unrivalled (Steve was the 1993 winner of the Palaeontological Association's Award to Amateur Palaeontologists, and the 1994 recipient of the Geological Society's R. H. Worth Prize). We arranged to visit the site on the Sunday and continue the excavation from where I had left off.
>
> On Sunday I arrived at the clay pit early in the morning, eager to start the work of clearing back the clay overburden. Much to my relief the site was just as I had left it on the Friday. I was soon joined by Steve Etches and between us we moved the clay back to reveal more of the skeleton. Some of the fragile bones were photographed and tagged before they were carefully lifted. This was necessary to protect them from further damage during the excavation. At least part of the post cranial skeleton was enclosed in a large limestone concretion covering an area of several metres. Bones found beyond the margin of the concretion had been crushed and distorted by the weight of the overlying sediment. The greatest surprise of the morning was the cranium; carefully uncovered by Steve, measuring almost six feet in length and lying to one side of the limestone concretion. Now that we had found the skull, we were able to confirm that the rest of the skeleton belonged to a pliosaur. We were both very excited as it was clear a substantial part of the skeleton lay before us, with who knew how much more awaiting discovery – a very rare and unusual find.
>
> Even after a full morning's work cutting back the clay with our tools, the skeleton was disappearing into the side of the clay pit. To rescue the pliosaur in its entirety would need a coordinated effort, many hands and materials and considerable expertise.

Deadly Doris

I contacted Peter Crowther at Bristol City Museum and updated him on our progress, in particular the discovery of the skull. The careful excavation of the pliosaur thereafter became the responsibility of his team from Bristol City Museum and Bristol University, and although the excavation continued for several more weeks, I was only able to assist very occasionally. The complexity of digging up a large and fragile skeleton required the expertise of the museum and university staff to ensure a successful excavation. When the partial skeleton had been completely uncovered it was parcelled in plaster and fiberglass jackets and transported in wooden crates to the Bristol Industrial Museum. From here it would travel to the City Museum and Art Gallery where the painstaking process of cleaning it would begin. Eventually the fully prepared remains would be exhibited at the Bristol City Museum and Art Gallery.

Simon's discovery would see him earn his fifteen minutes of fame, with it generating considerable media interest at local and even an international level. Various media outlets visited the site to conduct interviews with the people involved and the story was picked up by ITN, BBC West, HTV, Sky News, Radio 4, GWR, Wiltshire Sound, BBC World Service, *Daily Mail*, *The Guardian*, *Bristol Evening Post* and many more. It was big news!

The skeleton was identified as a new species of pliosaur – *Pliosaurus brachyspondylus* – by Dr Glenn Storrs of Bristol University. It was later renamed *Pliosaurus carpenteri* in honour of its discoverer and is one of the most complete specimens of its kind ever to be found.

Simon spent a period of twenty years collecting prehistoric remains from the Kimmeridge Clay sedimentary layer that the clay quarry excavation exposed. During that time, he has uncovered a rare turtle fossil, remains of plesiosaurs, ichthyosaurs, pliosaurs and crocodiles. He has also found the odd fish or two and a wing bone from a pterosaur.

During the excavation, the employees at the works christened the pliosaur 'Peter the pliosaur'. It was postulated that the specimen might be female, but it was later decided that there was not enough evidence to support this. However, for the narrative of the 2017 exhibition 'Pliosaurus! Face to Face with a Jurassic Beast', where the specimen would go on display, it was decided that it would be referred to as female.

Before Bristol Museum and Art Gallery was to put *Pliosaurus carpenteri* on display, a public vote was held to give her a name. The public chose to name the 150-million-year-old predator Doris. From June 2017 to February 2018, the public had the chance to come face to face with not only the skeleton that had taken Roger Vaughan, the geology conservator at the museum, ten painstaking years to clean and get to the stage where it could be displayed, but also a life-size, interactive model of 'Deadly Doris'.

Deborah Hutchinson, the current geology curator at the museum, highlights how important the discovery of Doris was:

The discovery of *Pliosaurus carpenter* is significant as the specimen is the first and currently the only known example of the species. The fossil is relatively complete and preserves many pathologies and injuries that gave us insight as to how this individual was living 150 million years ago.

Pliosaurus carpenteri wasn't the only big discovery made at the clay quarry. Another pliosaur was found in 1980 by visiting Danish geology students. This time only the skull and a few other elements were found, and it is on permanent display at Bristol Museum. This specimen was classified as *Pliosaurus westburyensis*.

The clay quarry offered only a small cross-sectional view of what life was like in the tropical seas during the Jurassic Period. From only the discoveries that the clay quarry revealed, it is clear that the seas were plentiful with an abundance of life. This small corner of Wiltshire, for a short and exciting period of time, helped give us a wonderful and valuable insight into what life was like 150 million years ago. This could not have been possible without the hard work and dedication of all those involved with the discovery and excavation of Doris and the co-operation of Blue Circle to allow and help with the excavation.

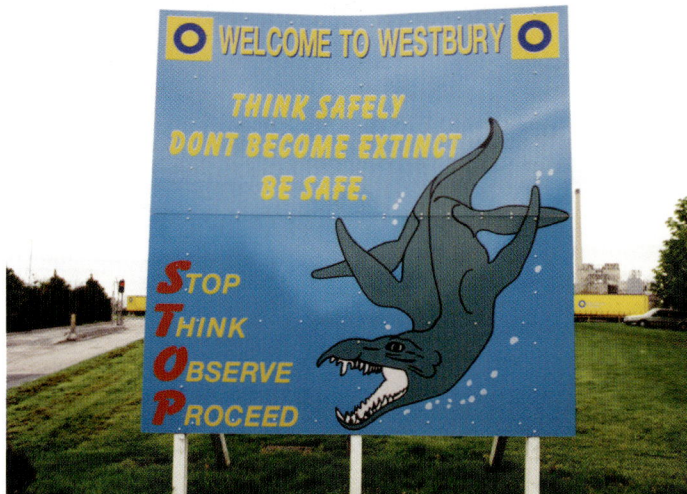

Left: This apt sign was placed at the entrance to the works in 1994.

Below: *Pliosaurus carpenteri* on display at Bristol Museum and Art Gallery in 2017. The fossilised skeleton was part of an educational and interactive display. (Photograph courtesy of Bristol Culture)

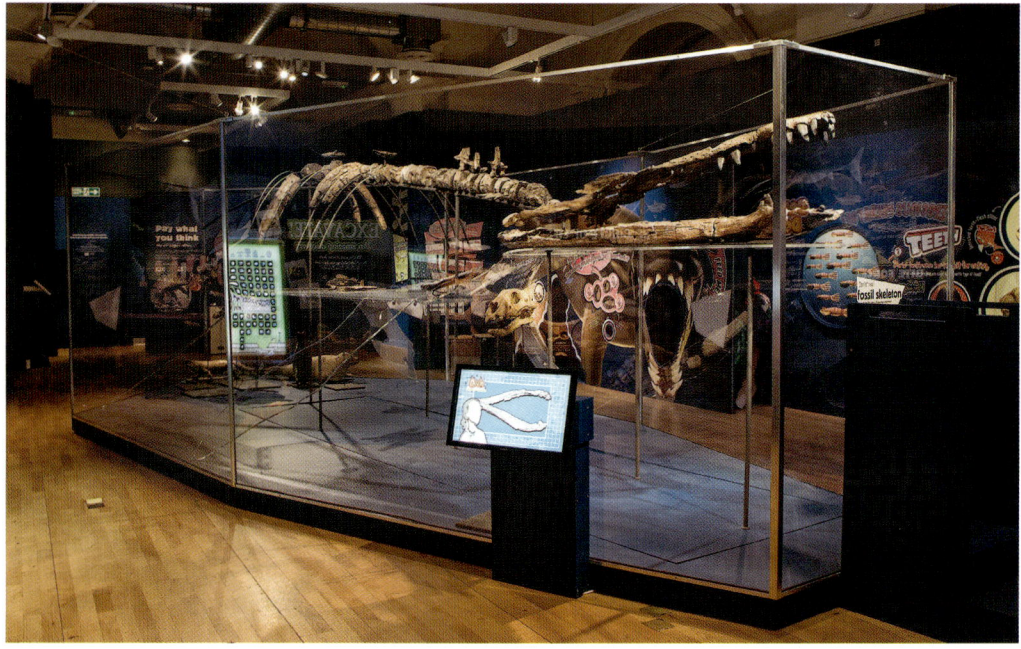

Deadly Doris

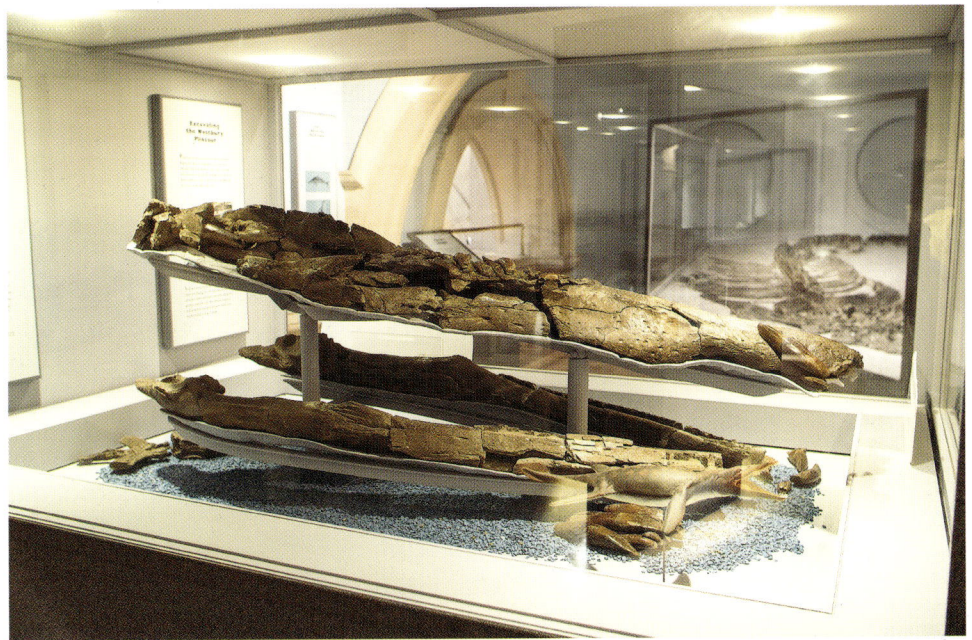

The skull of the first pliosaur, which was discovered in 1980. (Photograph courtesy of Bristol Culture)

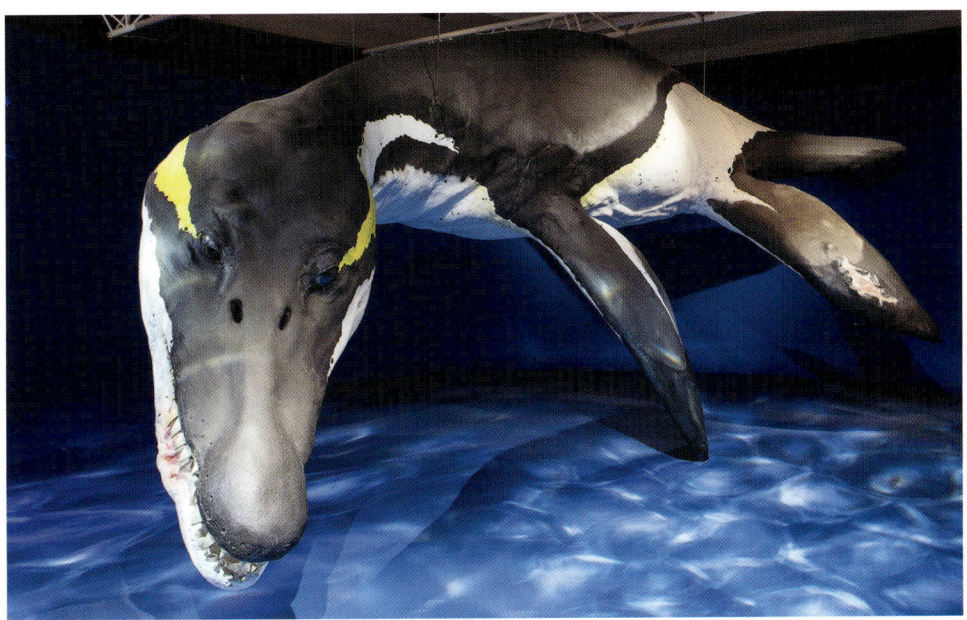

'Deadly Doris', the life-size model that was on display during the 2017 exhibition and is now on permanent display in Bristol Museum's back hall. She measured approximately 8 metres long and would have weighed approximately 4,500 kilograms. The wound on her hind flipper has been faithfully recreated from evidence that her fossilised bones revealed. (Photograph courtesy of Bristol Culture)

Chapter 9

Chimney Demolition

Sunday 18 September 2016, the morning that the chimney was demolished, is a morning that I think will remain fresh in my memory forever. We had an early start, having to be on site for a safety briefing from the explosives team at 4.30 a.m. Nerves and excited anticipation were responsible for very little sleep the night before – I had spent most of the night running through how I hoped the morning would play out.

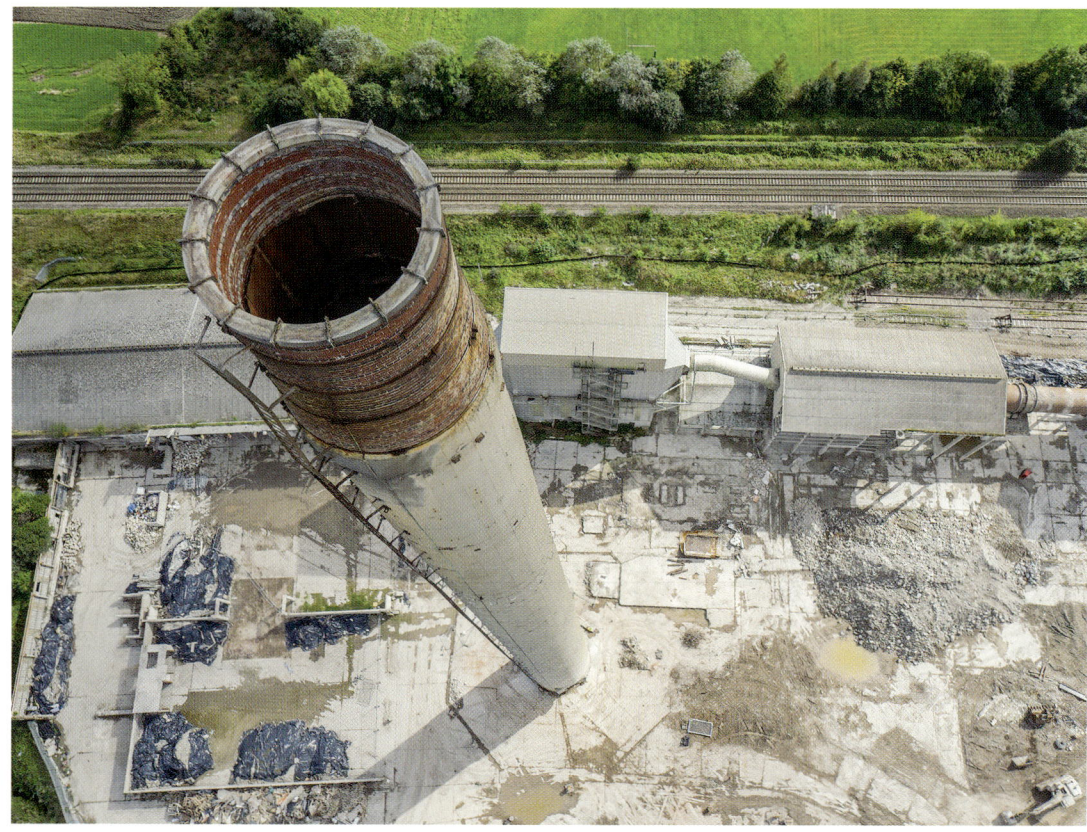

Looking down from just under 500 feet.

Chimney Demolition

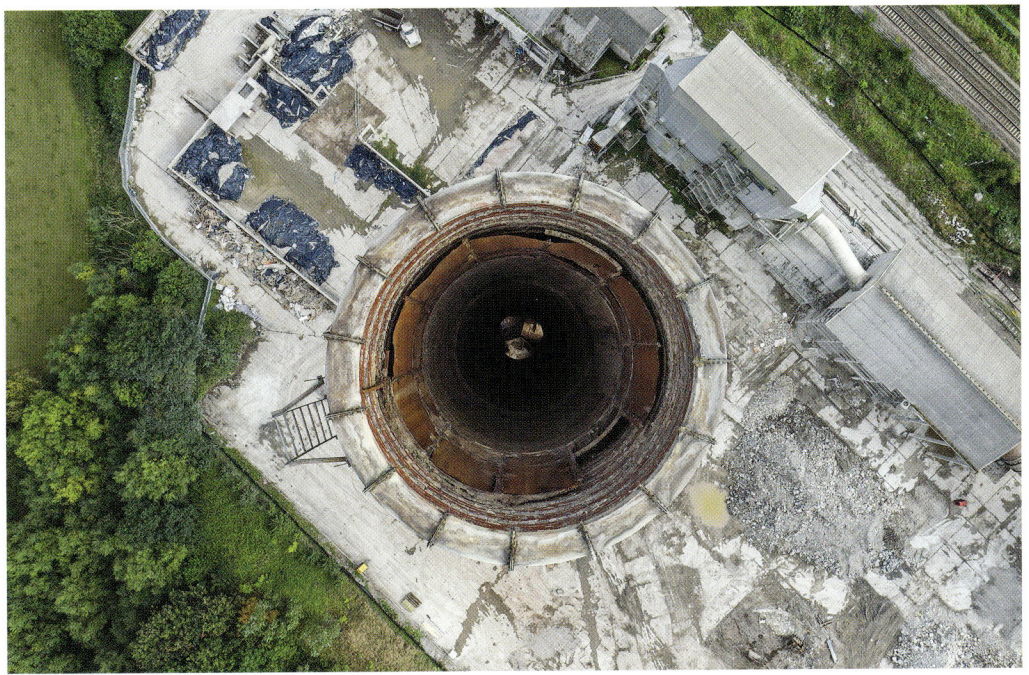

Looking directly down the 400-foot chimney. Light shines through holes that were cut in the base just before the chimney's demolition.

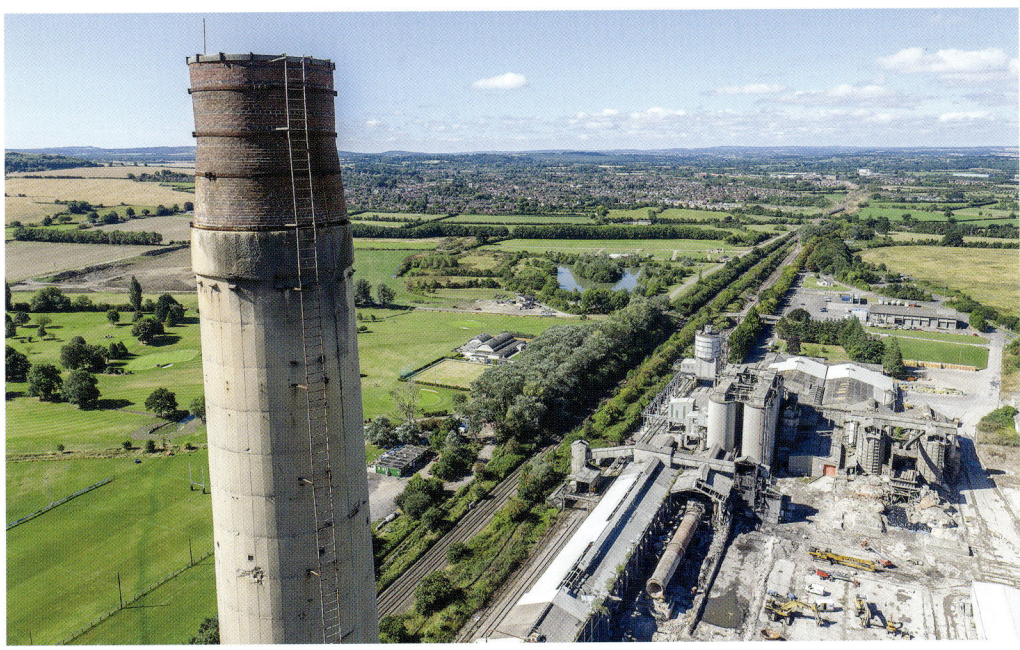

As the railway stretches to Westbury, the crumbling concrete on the chimney is clearly visible. Had the works stayed operational, the chimney would have had to have been repaired at a cost of around £40,000.

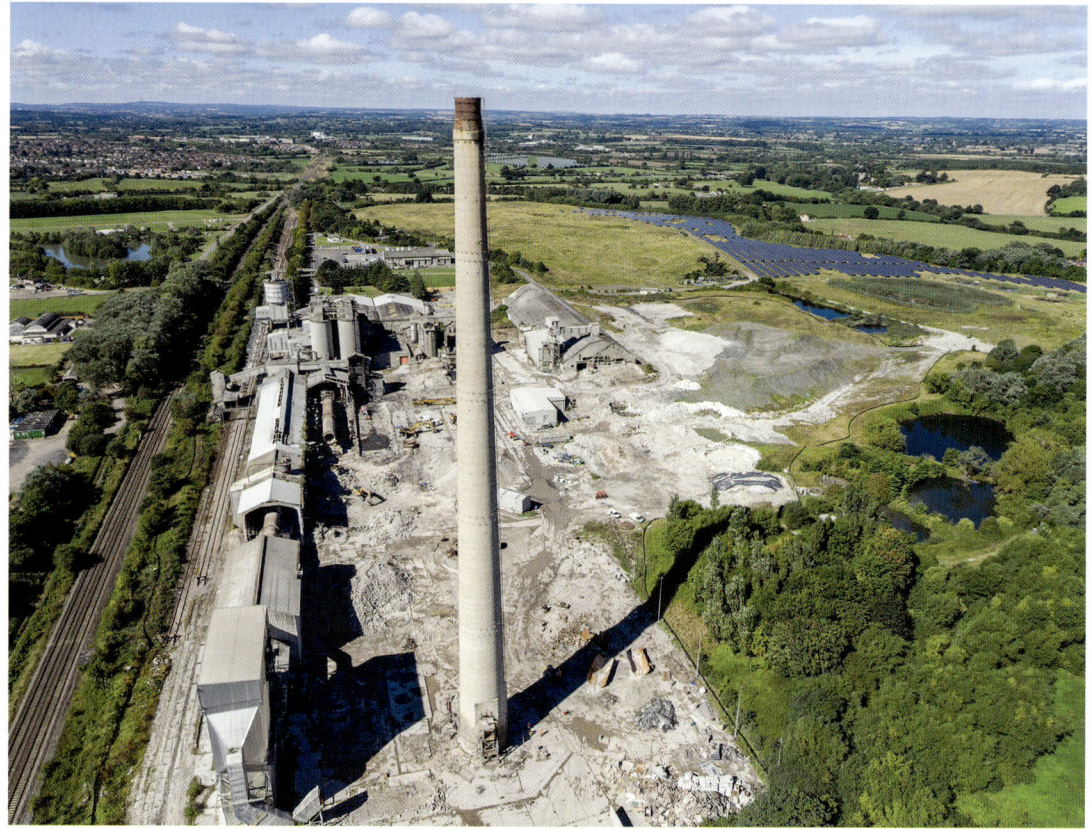

Taken at 11.05 a.m., just three weeks before the demolition of the chimney, its shadow casts almost the exact path where it will later come to rest.

The official timeline that everybody was working to on the morning of the demolition went as follows:

T – 1hr 30min   Brief sentries and test radios. Network Rail confirm clear to proceed with blow down. Note: extra sentries and radios to be available if required.

T – 1hr 10min   Establish exclusion zone with lookouts in place and evacuate all site personnel with the exception of the explosives team at the firing point. Coordination meeting with control team to go ahead with firing at firing point.

T – 1hr   Railway closure/timing confirmed.

T – 45min   Area check complete radio check.

T – 30min   Coordinating meeting at control point. Radio check.

Chimney Demolition

T – 15min	All personnel less firing team evacuate zone. Public footpaths confirmed closed. Railway to confirm line clear. Final connections.
T – 10min	Clearance checklist completed by all agencies. Granted NWR clearance to proceed.
T – 5min	One minute continuous warning siren. Confirm temporary footpaths clear and closed off with red bunting tape. Confirm all OK with Network Rail representative. Final radio checks to all sentries.
T – 30sec	Warning maroon.
T (7 a.m.)	Blow down.
T plus 5min	Explosive team inspects demolished structure and ensure all charges have detonated.
T plus 10min	Sound intermittent 'All Clear' siren and re-open footpath. Network Rail line inspected. Lookouts return to site.

Working to a timeline like this was great. It meant that we all knew exactly what was going to happen and when. This was especially important as we had limited flight times with the two drones. We therefore knew that we could take off five minutes before the 7 a.m. blow down, which would give us time to get the drones into position and make sure the cameras on them were recording.

After our safety briefing we had nothing to do but hang around for an hour in the cold. I didn't like this period of inactivity as it only helped to increase my nerves. I would much rather have been busy doing something; having something specific to focus on would have distracted me from the nervous tension that was building within me. Although I was confident that everything would work as planned with myself and Peter operating the drones, Andy entering the exclusion zone to set up the GoPros and Louis acting as an observer keeping an eye on the airspace, the nervous tension wouldn't dissipate. I had put a lot of pressure on myself to not mess this up. Even though there was still more demolition of the site to cover after the chimney was gone, for me the past few months had been building up to this one moment. We had to get it right!

Then the power on site was turned off and we stood around in darkness. A break in the clouds revealed stars that would soon be giving way to the dawn light. One shone far brighter than the others and was moving – it was the International Space Station passing directly overhead. I'm not really superstitious, but I took the passing flight of the ISS to be a good omen. I watched as it passed over us in southerly direction and it slowly faded into the black over the White Horse, where hundreds of people would soon be gathered.

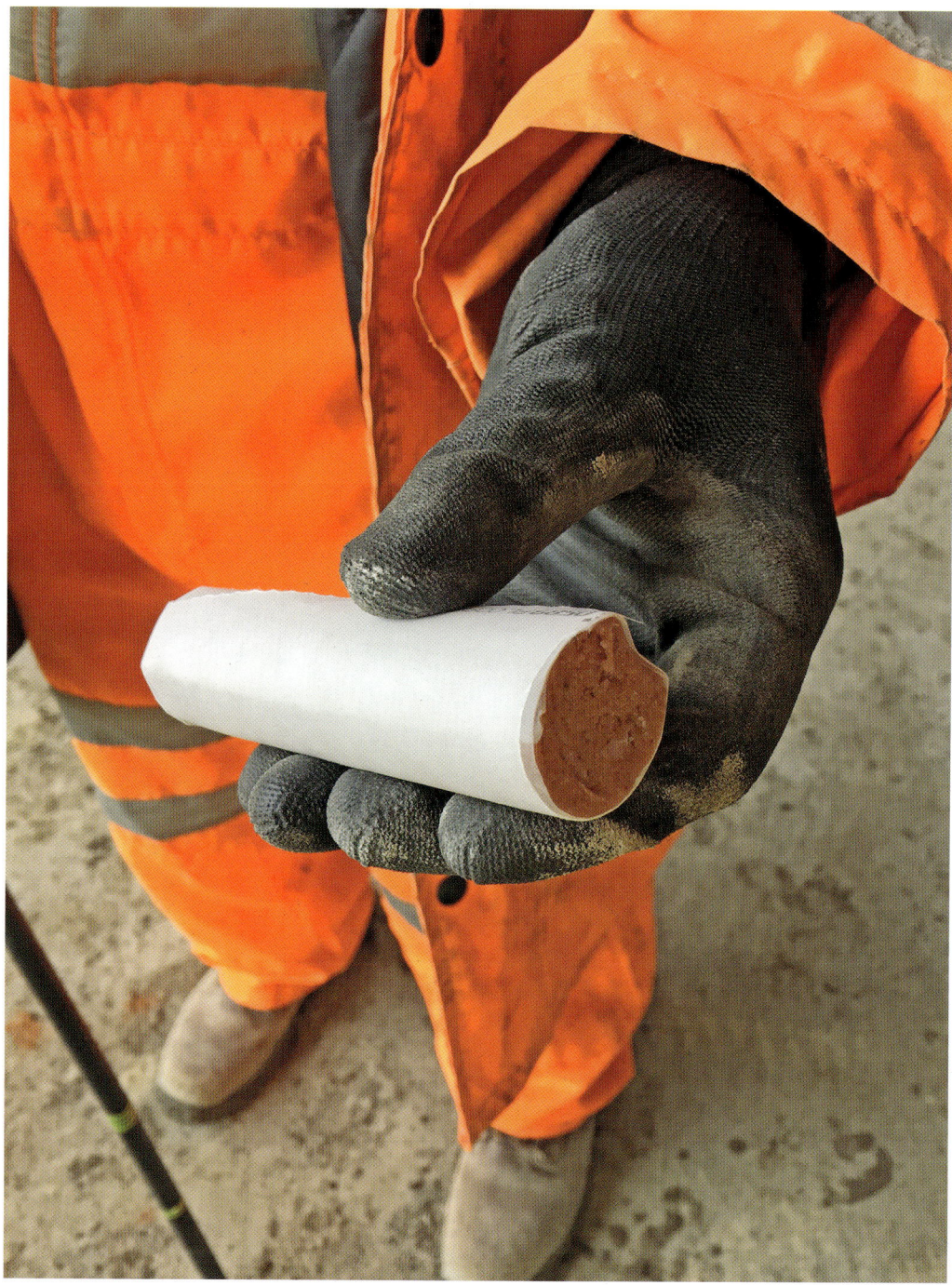
One of the many cylinders of Gelignite explosive that were planted into the inside wall of the chimney base. Around 15 kilograms in total of this explosive were used.

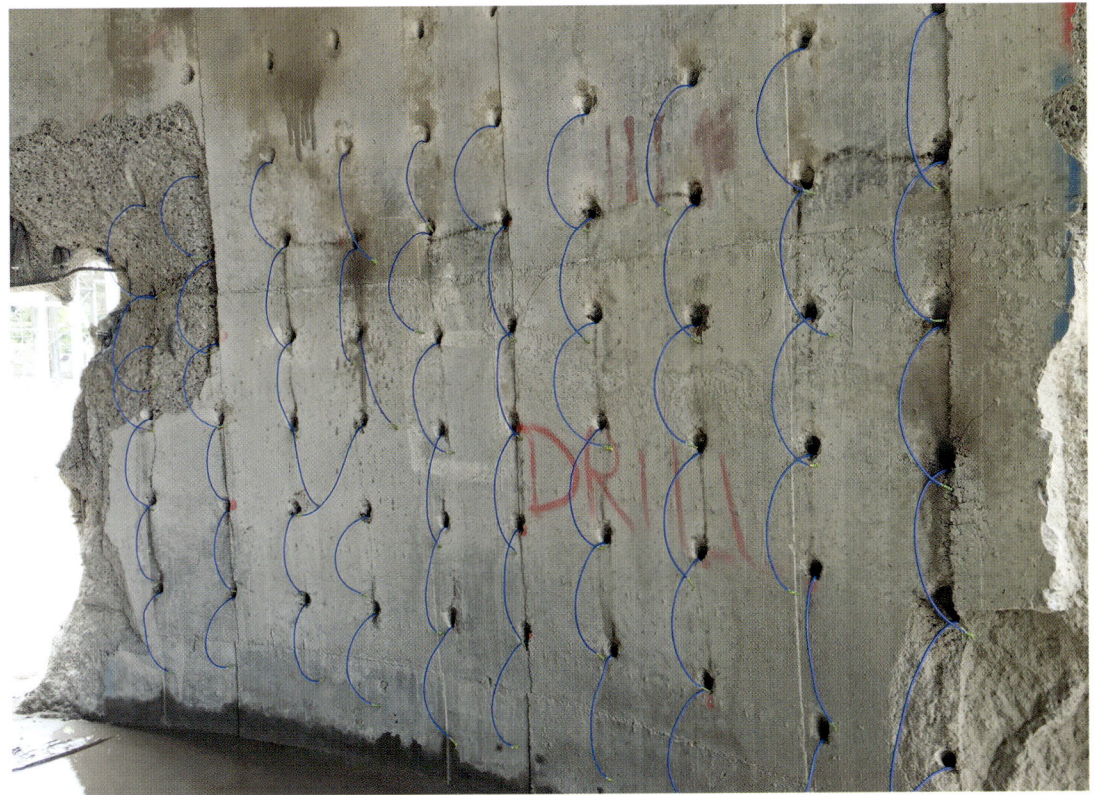

The detonation cord attached to the explosives in the chimney wall.

Six o'clock finally came and it was time for myself and Andy to enter the 360-meter exclusion zone to turn on the cameras. I was escorted up to the top of the silos to set a camera up on its tripod, while Andy was escorted to the precipitator just behind the chimney to turn on the first GoPro and then over to the second GoPro, which was situated near the ponds – as close as we could get to where the top of the chimney would fall.

Andy was one of the last few people to ever stand under the chimney. Later he would tell me that he was far more focused on the fact that it was loaded with explosives, rather than how much of an historic moment it was!

I scaled the stairs to the top of the silos and reached my tripod. The atmosphere was like nothing I had experienced before during my numerous visits to the cement works. From the top of the silos you get a beautiful view of the chimney, and even though it was still quite dark, I could still make out its towering, ghostly form. The base of the chimney was being warmly illuminated by the glow of the vehicle headlamps of the explosives team. There was an almost eerie silence that shrouded the entire site. I had never experienced the place so quiet. Then to my right, I noticed the traffic jam of car headlights up on the escarpment of the White Horse. So many cars! During meetings in the weeks before this day the question had been asked – 'How many people will turn up to watch?' Now we knew – it was a lot! Some people had even spent the night camping in their cars so that they could get a front-row view!

There was a very special person in among the crowd that was gathering up on the hill. Lily Sargent had entered a colouring competition that Tarmac had organised. Her picture was chosen as the winner and now she was waiting excitedly in the darkness at the front of the gathering crowd. Her prize was to activate an explosives plunger when the countdown to the chimney detonation reached zero.

My focus returned to setting the camera up – just as the warning siren was tested. In an instant, the silence and my nerves were shattered. It frightened the life out of me! And in that one instant, it hit me – this was really happening! OK Simon, don't mess this up!

Back down on the ground the drones were set up as my nerves continued to increase. I had written our own timetable to make our lives easier and our 6.55 a.m. take-off time was fast approaching. I knew that I only needed around one minute to get my drone into position, but Peter would need longer. So, at 6.50 a.m. I told Peter to power up and get in the air. As soon as he cleared the take-off area I powered up the other drone. I watched as Peter flew the drone out over the clinker shed, and as it turned into a small black dot nearing its 340-meter distant parking spot I then took off to get into position. Acting as observer for Peter, Andy helped him frame the shot. Louis was my observer and soon spotted a stray drone entering our air space. I think that it may have spotted my drone as it did back off, so thankfully it didn't ruin our shots.

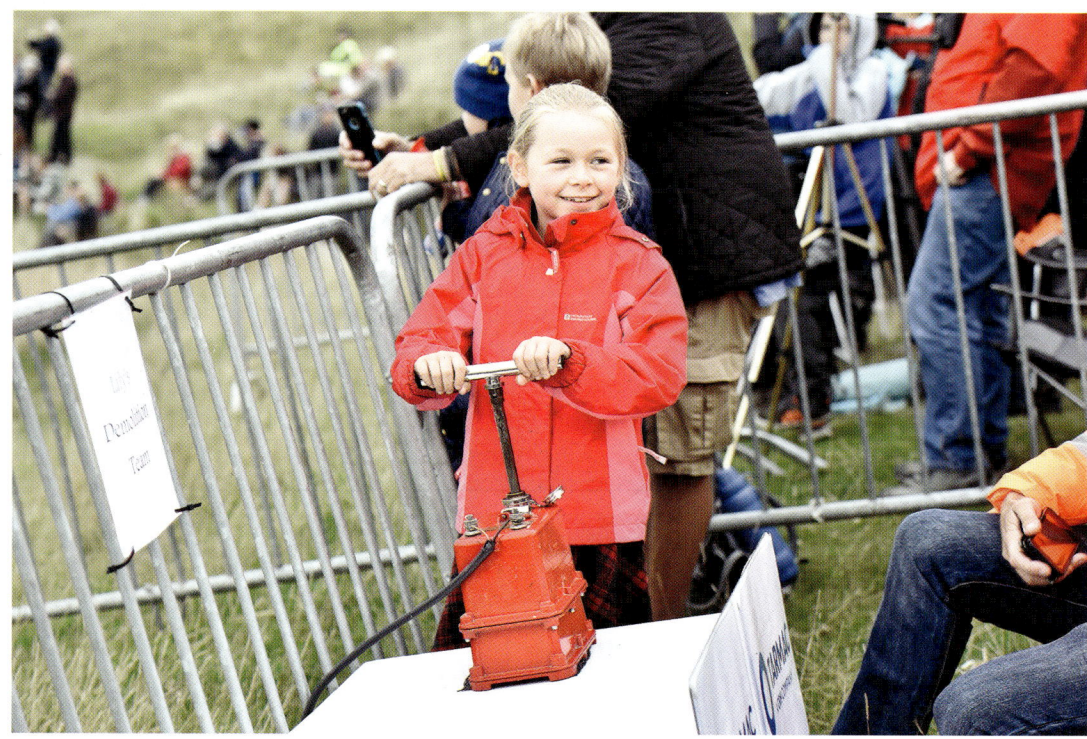

Lily posing for pictures on the morning of the demolition. (Copyright Diane Vose Wiltshire Times)

Chimney Demolition

At T minus thirty seconds we heard the warning maroon ignite, but we never saw it. It turns out that it just flew along the ground instead of up towards the chimney! This was a relief for me, because even though the explosives team knew where the drones would be parked and had assured me that they wouldn't get hit by the warning maroon, part of me was still worried that one of the drones would get hit. At this point I was constantly checking the aircraft and glancing down at my iPad to ensure that the shot was framed correctly, that the camera was recording, and that everything was doing what it should be doing – we were only getting one shot at this!

Then, at 7 a.m. we heard the words 'fire now, fire now', and at around fifteen seconds after 7 a.m. the Westbury skyline was forever changed.

There was a loud crack from the long detonation cord and then a very loud bang from the Gelignite explosives in the base of the chimney. This moment also signalled the end of the resident peregrine falcons' favourite perch, the explosion in the base of the chimney sending both birds flying. Time then seemed to come to a crawl as the chimney slowly bowed out of existence. From our location (we couldn't see the base of the chimney) it looked to me for a couple of seconds as if nothing had happened. What we would later be able to discern from one of the GoPros was that first the chimney fell a few degrees, then it dropped into itself for a couple of feet before continuing to slowly fall to a perfect landing. Concrete and steel rebar that had withstood the elements for fifty-one years creaked and cracked as the chimney gracefully fell. As it neared a 45-degree angle, the top red brick section could no longer hold on to the concrete that it had been anchored to. The bulk of the chimney accelerated towards the ground, briefly overtaking the top brick section as they separated. The main concrete section hit the ground, followed by the red bricks that were partly hidden in their own dust. In a last dying breath, two huge blasts of dusty air were expelled from the base. Then there was silence.

It went exactly as planned and I'll never forget the sound when it hit the ground. From our vantage point the sound reverberated around the buildings and sounded like a cross between the loudest slap you've ever heard and a clap of thunder.

I had enough flight time left in my drone to keep it in the air as the dust settled. As I flew toward the chimney a thin layer of dust hung in the air like a veil, trying to conceal the destruction that lay beneath. I really don't know what I was expecting to see, but to my surprise the chimney was relatively intact – albeit rather flat now. Much of the base was still its original cylindrical shape and looked to be in reasonable condition. The rest of the chimney, however, now resembled a road that had just been laid across the site. It was a sad, but somewhat impressive sight.

Back up on the White Horse, Lily and her parents were now looking at a view that was now not so familiar. As the dust hung over the fallen chimney in the still morning air, Lily was left with a memory that she will likely never forget:

> I had won the chance to blow up the chimney from entering a local colouring competition and out of 600 pictures I was so excited that they picked mine as the winner! I felt so nervous and excited on the morning of the demolition that I had butterflies in my tummy, especially when I heard all the hundreds of people, including my family and friends, stood up on the White Horse next to me shouting the countdown – ten, nine, eight, seven, six, five, four, three, two, one! Then it was all down to me to push the plunger. Boom!

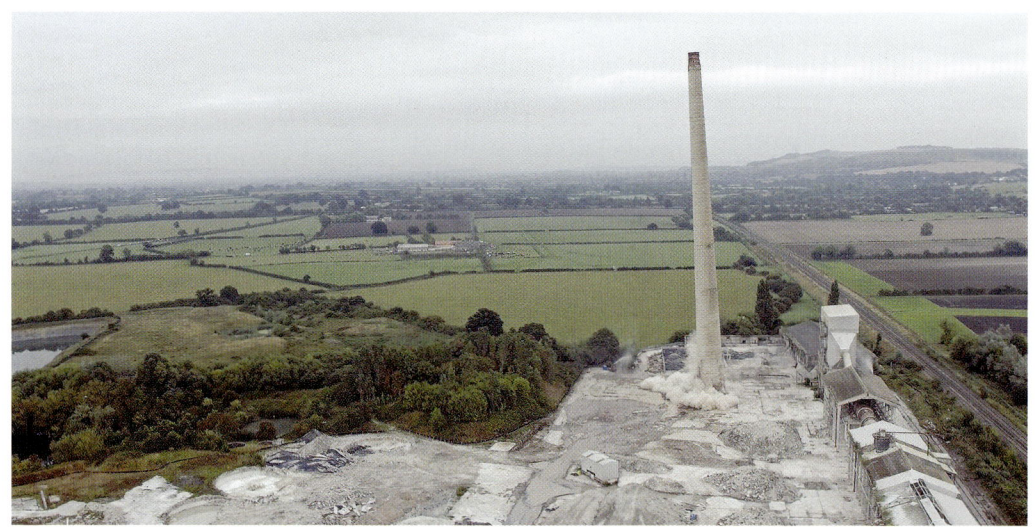

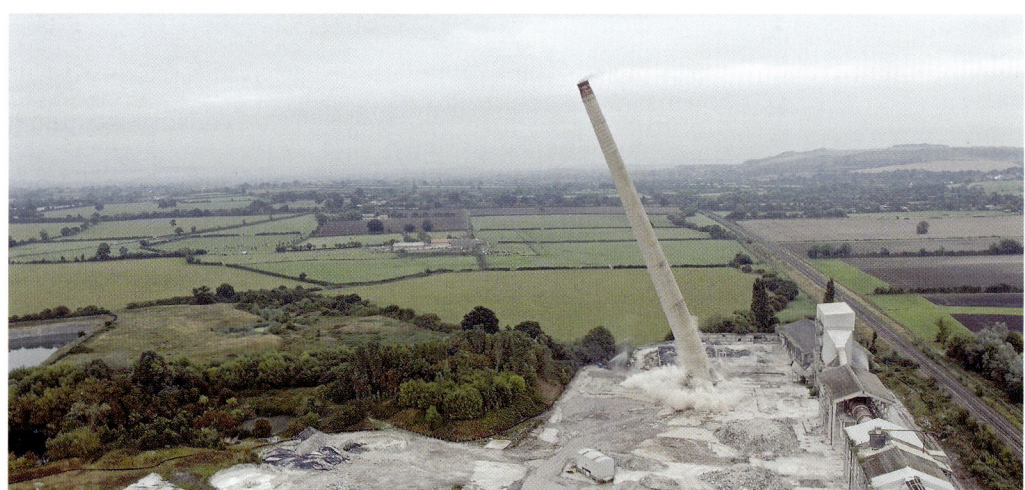

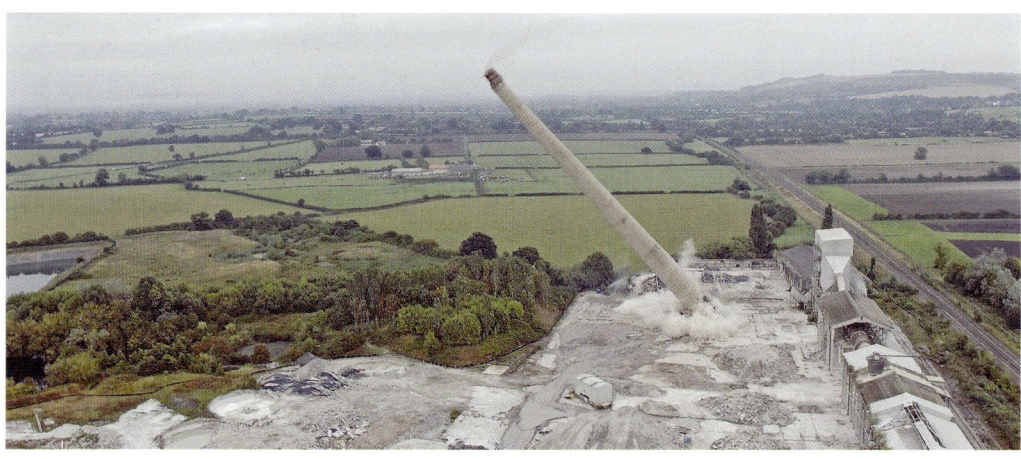

Chimney Demolition

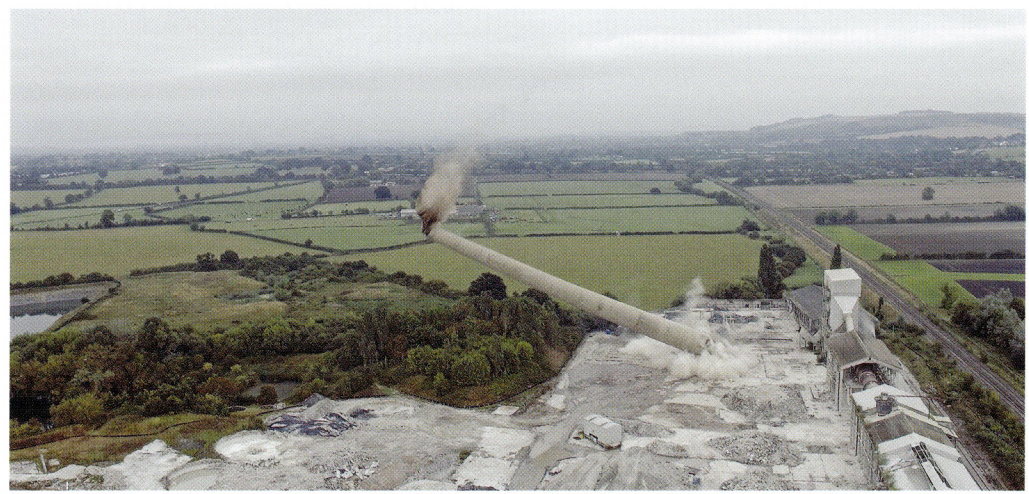

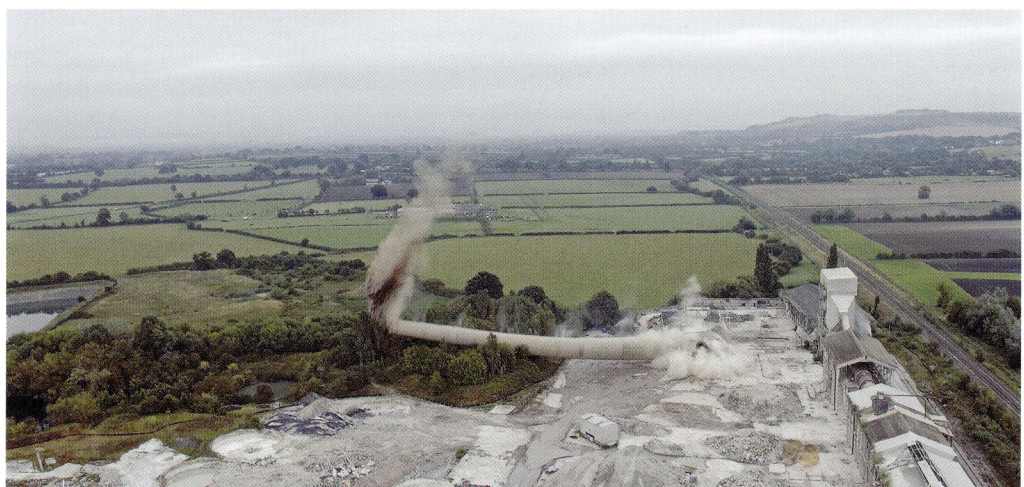

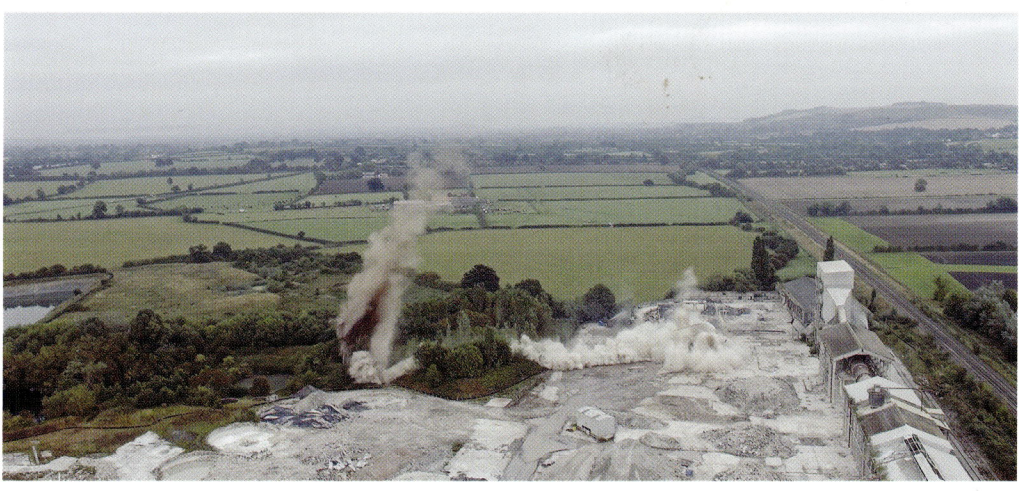

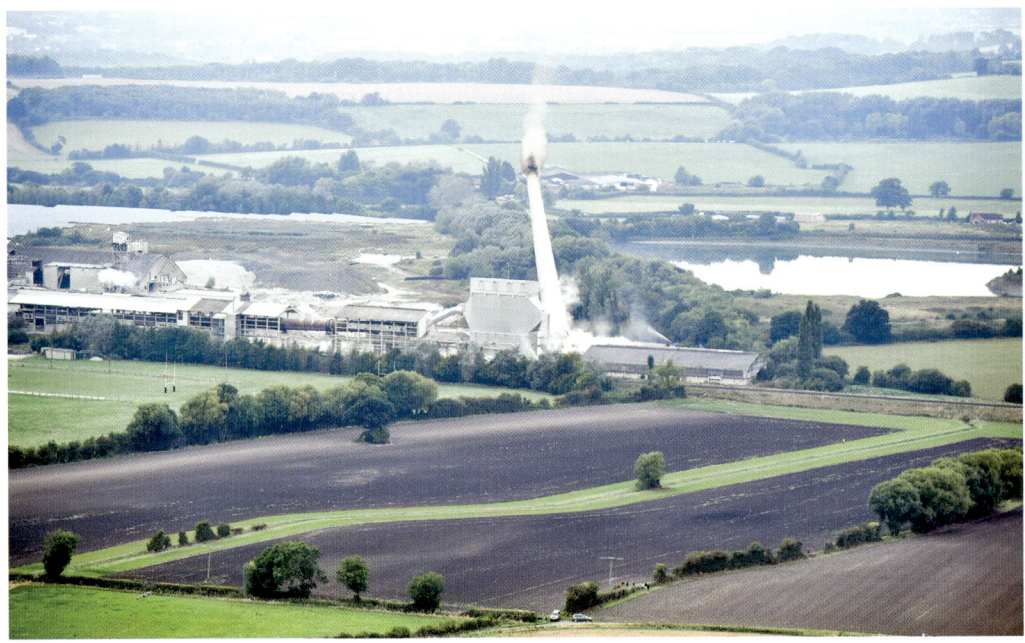

The view from the White Horse. (Copyright Diane Vose Wiltshire Times)

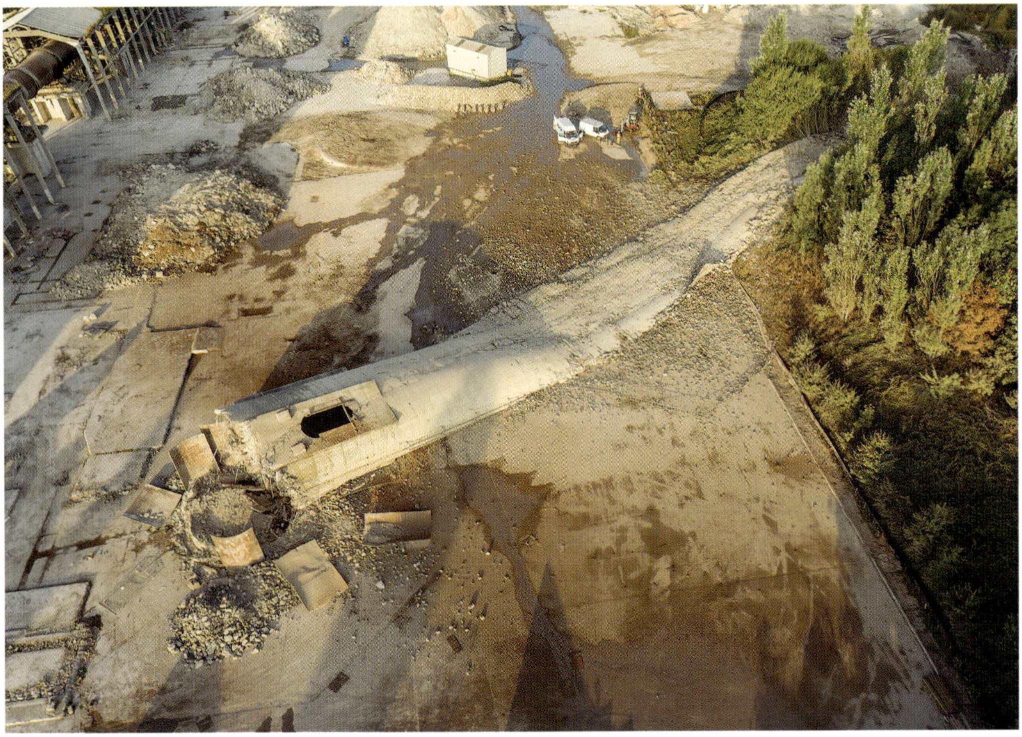

Pipefix was one of the first companies on site, checking for any damage that the impact may have caused to the mains water supply.

Chimney Demolition

Now the race was on to pack up our equipment that we had around the site so that we could re-locate closer to the chimney after the all clear had been given. We had to get some video and still imagery of the fallen chimney, so we moved to the clay stock pile where we could more safely and easily fly along the length of the chimney. After a dull and overcast morning, the sun now came out to add a touch of warmth to the last aerial shots we would get of the chimney. It was a perfect ending to an unforgettable morning.

I went back to the works on Monday morning and it was very strange approaching the site with the chimney no longer on the skyline. I think that pretty much every time I had driven to Westbury I had looked for the chimney, and it was very strange now that it wasn't there. Until I had started covering the demolition, the chimney never meant anything to me. It used to fascinate me because it was so tall, but that was about it. If you had have asked me before I started the project if I would miss the chimney when it was down, I would have laughed at you and said, 'Don't be silly, it's only a chimney!' But now, having spent so much time close to it, photographing and filming it, I guess I did miss it.

Some people were glad to see it come down, but I think more people were sad to see it go. It was a symbol of a big, important company that had lots of history behind it. It's all too easy to say that a building or a structure is a scar on the landscape, and maybe the chimney was. But what is often forgotten is that sometimes these structures are a necessity – they have to be built somewhere.

Walking down past the clinker shed and approaching the chimney that now lay horizontally out across the site was quite sad for me. The landmark that could once be

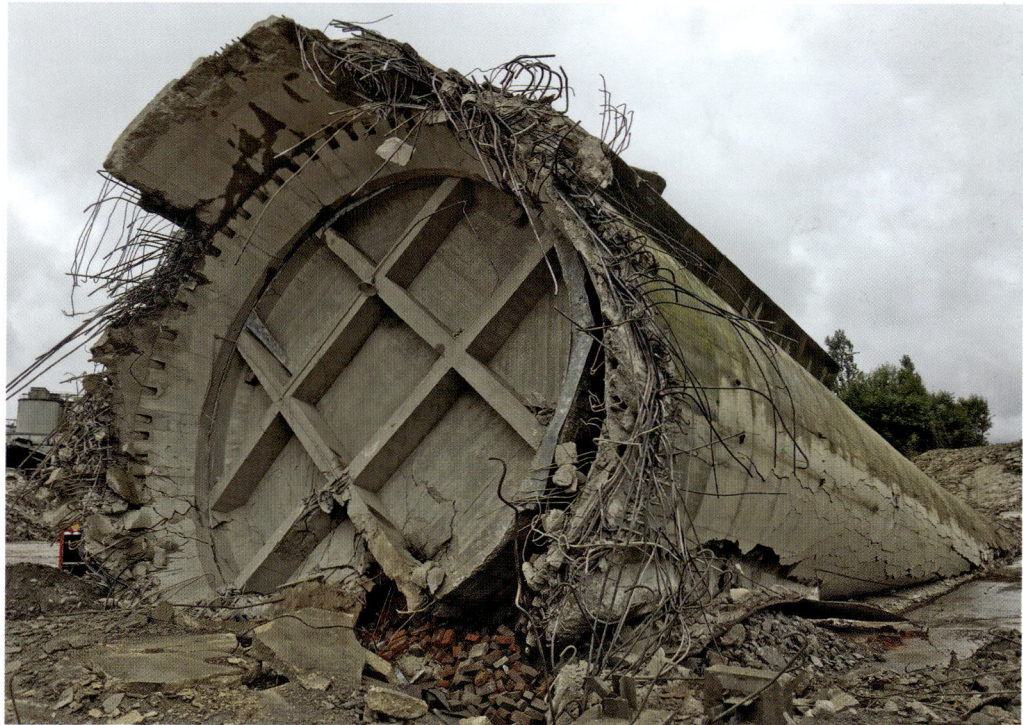

The base of the fallen chimney.

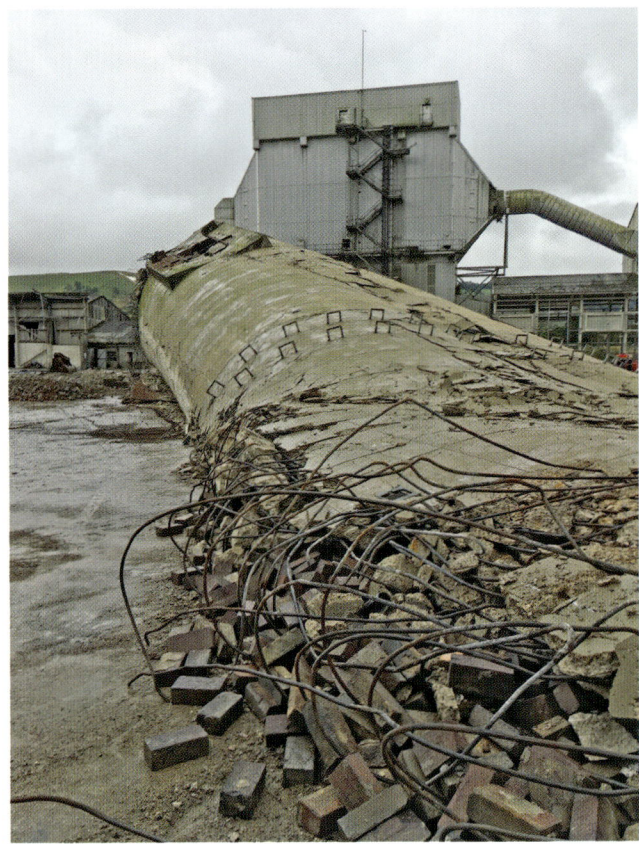

Insulating bricks and rebar spill from its ruptured side.

seen from miles around was now on the ground before me, its reinforcing steel rebar skeleton visible through the fractured mass of concrete. The inner skin of insulating bricks that had not been seen since the chimney's construction, which had started back in 1964, now spilled out of its ruptured sides; the ceiling inside the base that was above my head only two days before now lay exposed; a tangled mess of rebar that once helped anchor it to the ground was protruding from its sides like the roots of a huge upturned tree; a landmark that had once signalled the near completion of many local resident's homeward-bound journeys was now waiting to be pulverised to dust.

There were many more visits to the works after the chimney fell. The demolition of the chimney did give me a slight feeling of finality to the project, but there were still many more buildings and structures to be demolished. With the chimney gone, the second precipitator could be brought to the ground. All 500 feet of Kiln No. 2 was still present, as was the clinker shed, the mill house and refuse plant. As winter of 2016 slowly started to tighten its grip, more of the works was pulled to the ground, cut up, crushed and transported off site to be recycled.

I spent many hours stood in the cold and the rain, watching the sole remaining kiln being cut up and pulled from its concrete plinths. The second to last section didn't give up without a fight; it took three excavators – one pulling and two pushing – before it slid from its pier in a shower of sparks in the fading evening light. The large steel tire that had refused to be parted from its two rollers hit the ground with a loud metallic 'ting', with the force of the impact splitting it into two. Out of all the steel tires on both kilns, this was the only one to break upon hitting the ground. Had the works remained operational, this steel tire would have likely soon needed to be replaced.

Once the last kiln had been removed, it was then on to the clinker shed and mill house. At this stage of the demolition the site had been completely levelled, and it did somewhat resemble a war zone, with plenty of rubble and metalwork lying around. Come spring of 2017 the site had been cleared, and the offices, packing plant and storage silos aside, what remained was approximately 17 acres of flat concrete.

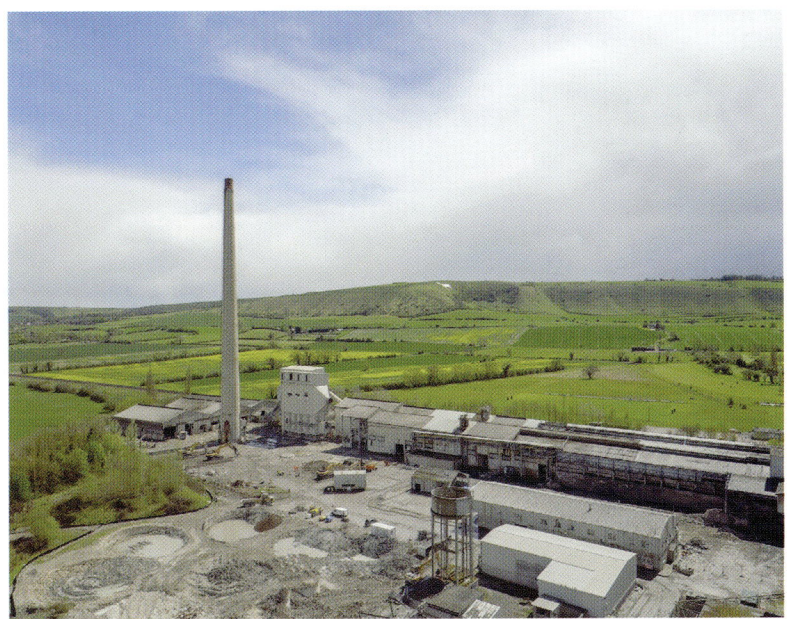

Preparing to pull over precipitator number one. 26 April 2016.

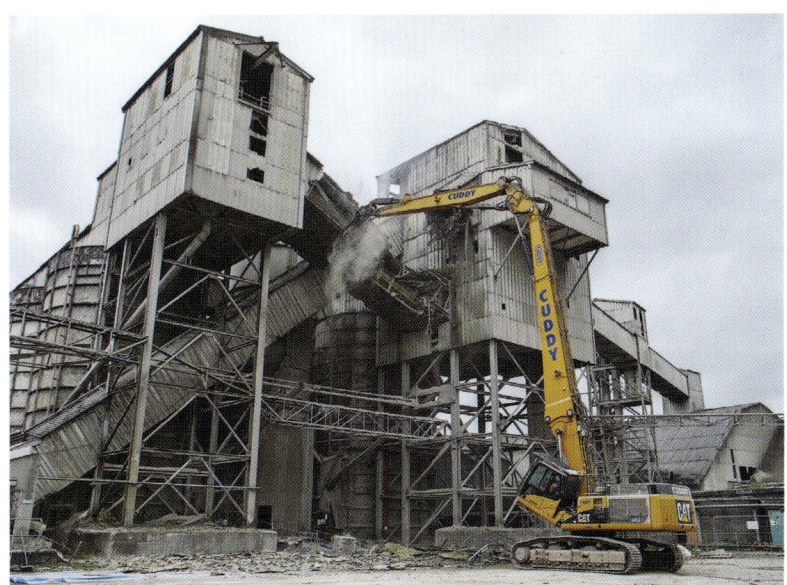

Demolition of the clinker conveyors. 17 May 2016.

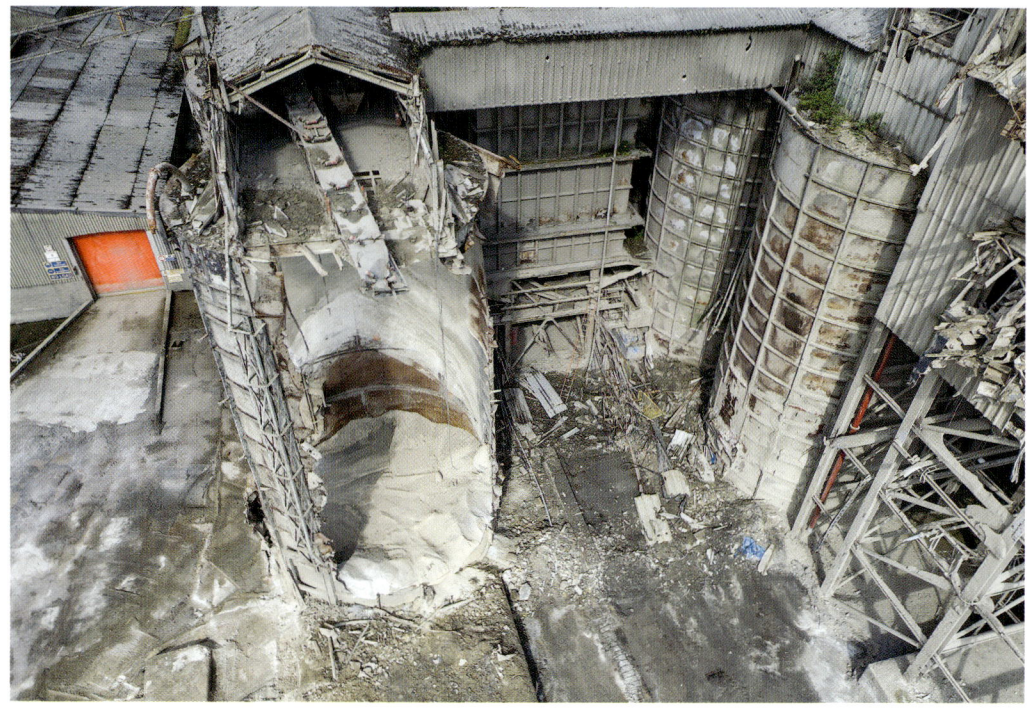

The clinker and gypsum silo demolition. Around 500 to 600 tons of product was left in each silo. 18 June 2016.

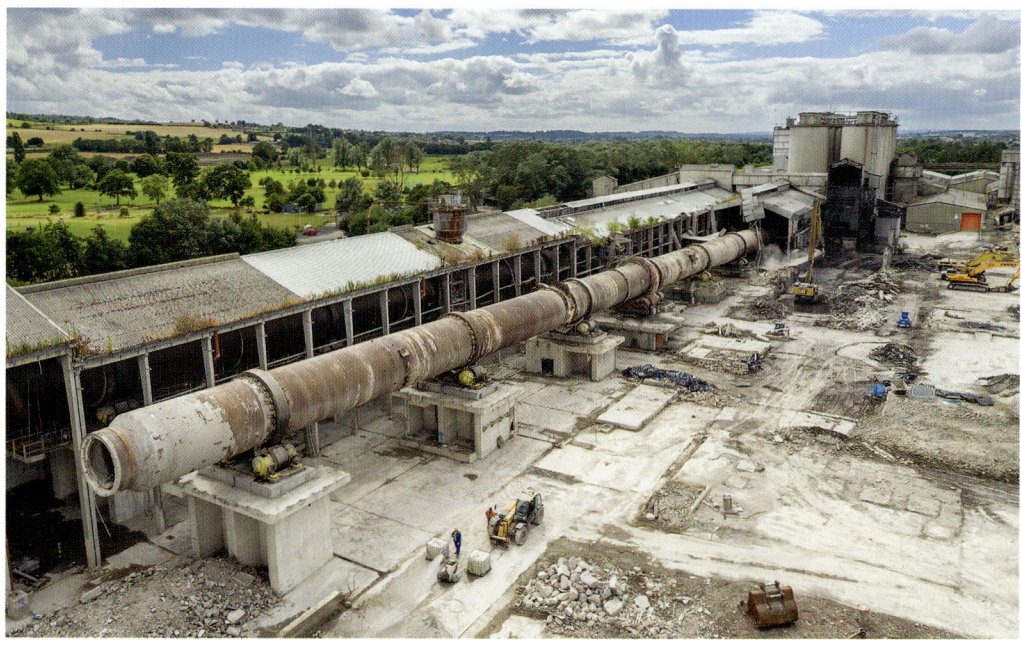

Kiln No. 1 is almost completely exposed, with work still ongoing at the front end of the building. 3 August 2016.

Chimney Demolition

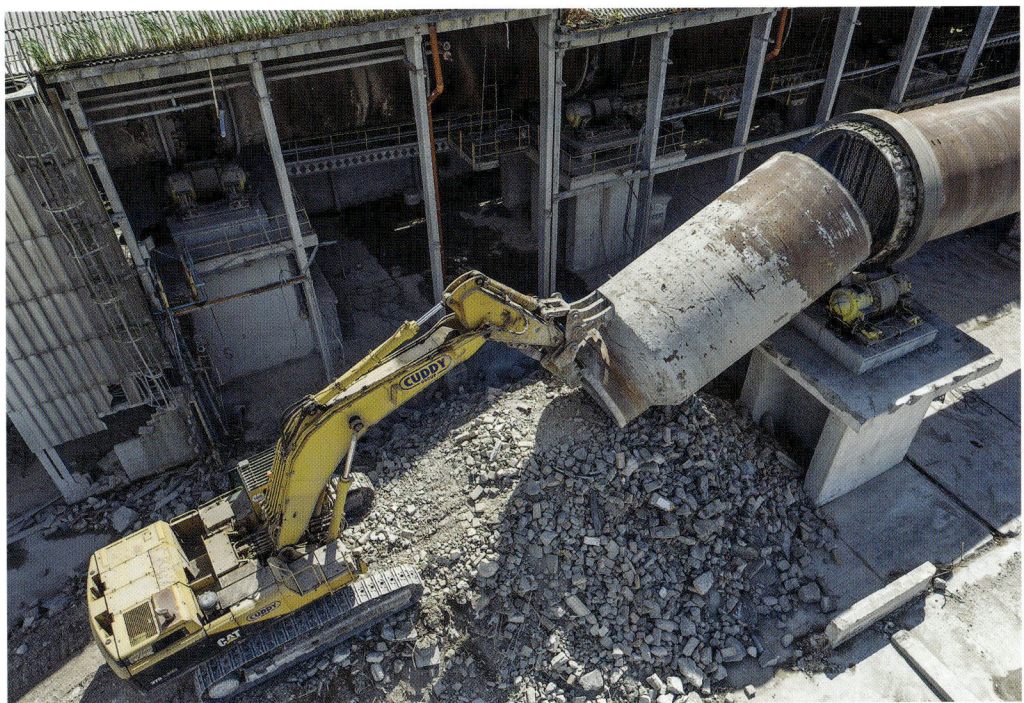

The chains in the back end of the kiln are visible now that the first section has been dropped. 4 August 2016.

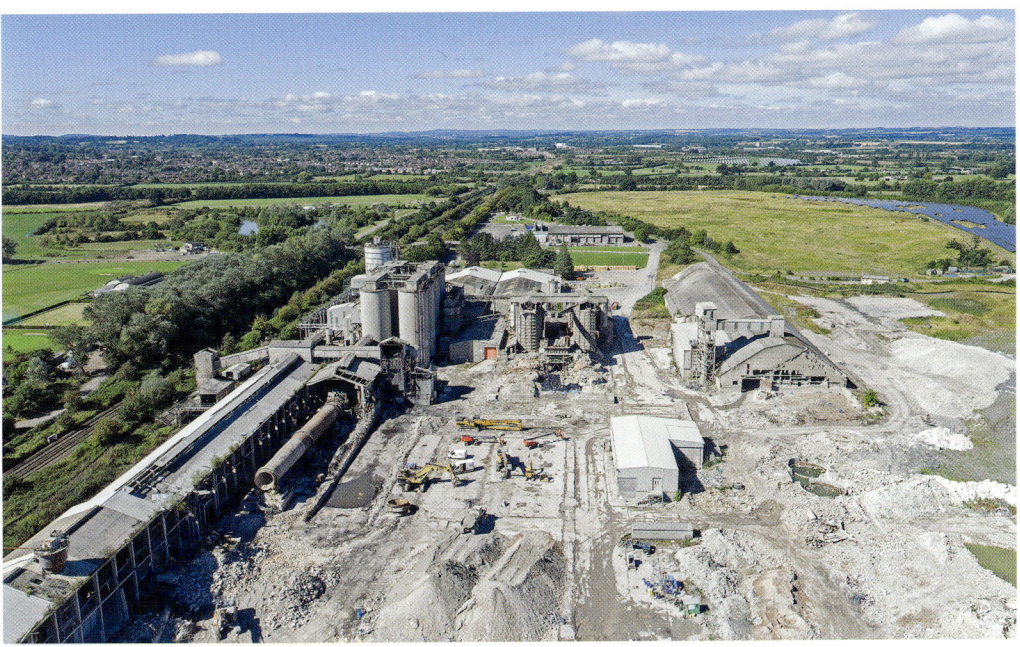

Just two sections of Kiln No. 1 remain. Clinker from the silos is being piled up in the foreground. 26 August 2016.

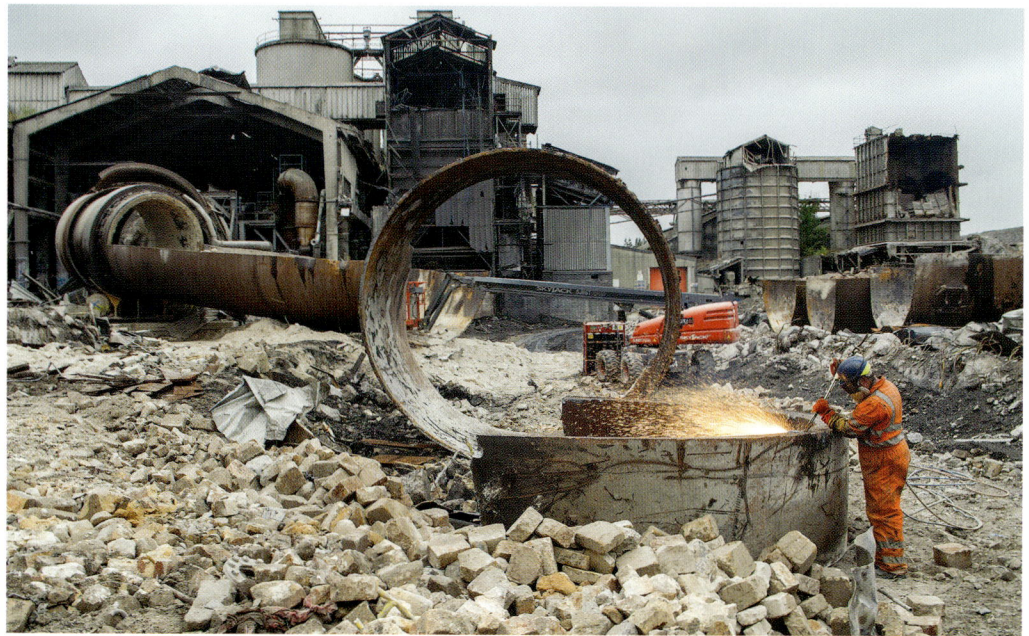

The last section of Kiln No. 1 being dissected. 5 September 2016.

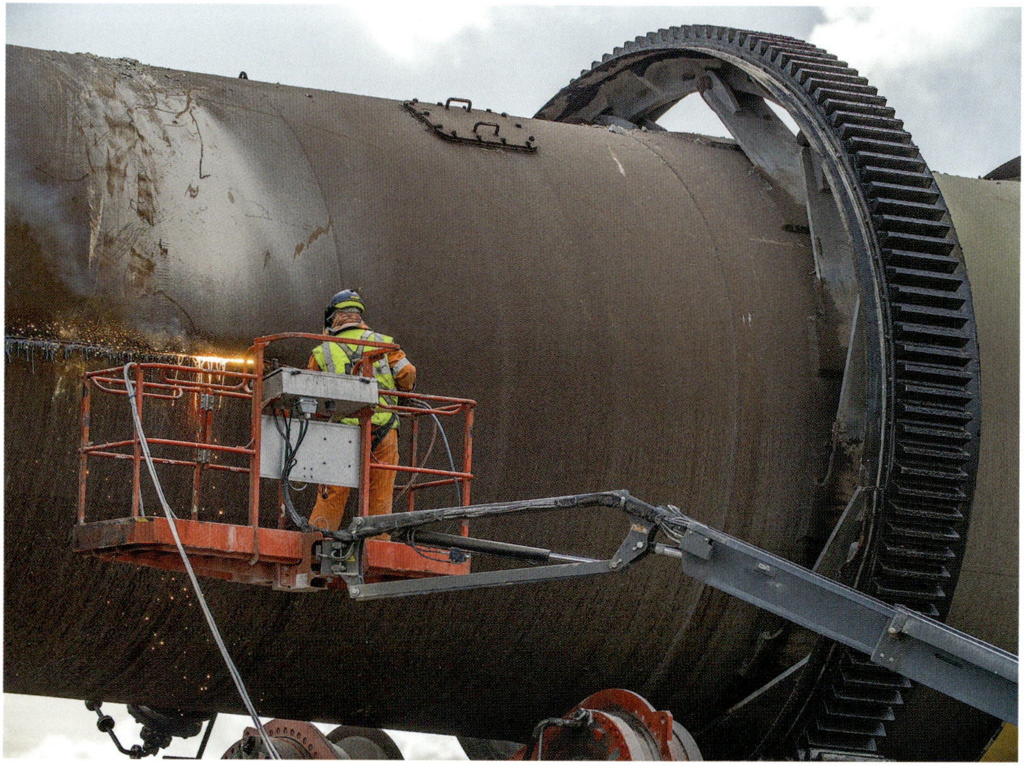

The shell of Kiln No. 2 is being cut just in front of its huge drive gear. 10 October 2016.

Chimney Demolition

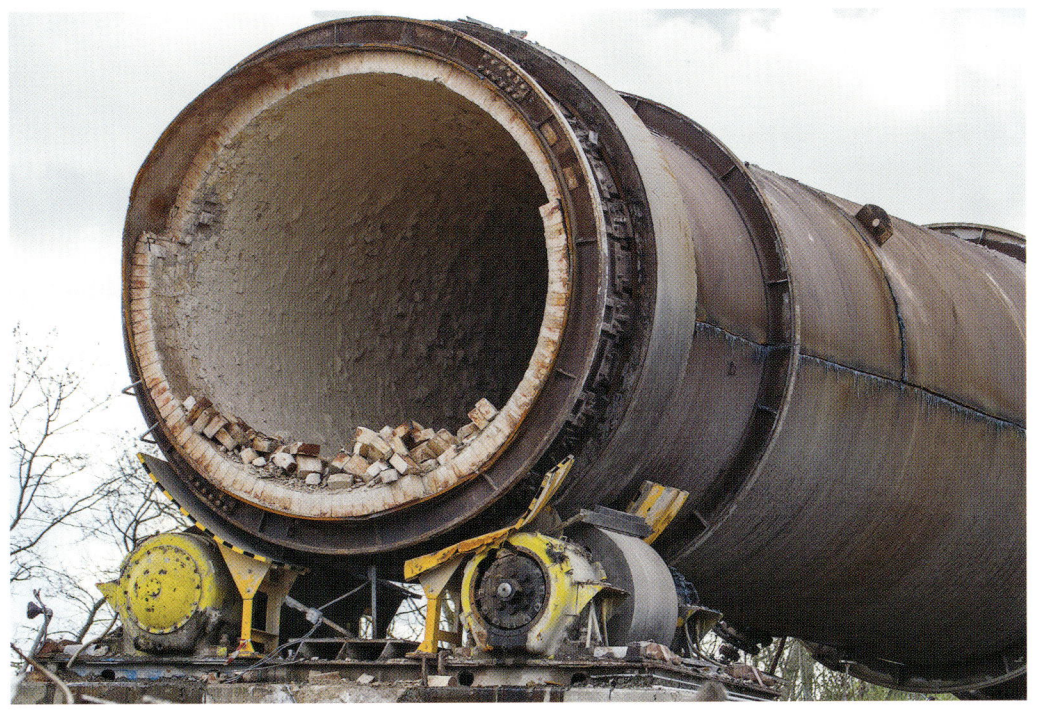

The insulating fire bricks lining the inside of Kiln No. 2. 10 October 2016.

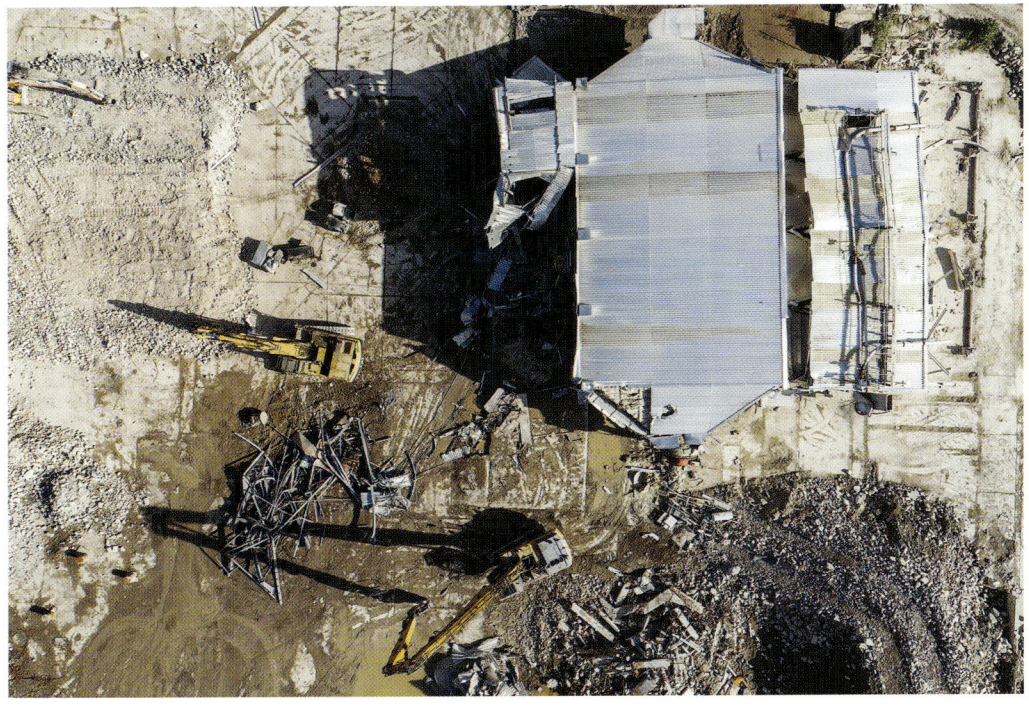

Precipitator No. 2 pulled to the ground. 18 October 2016.

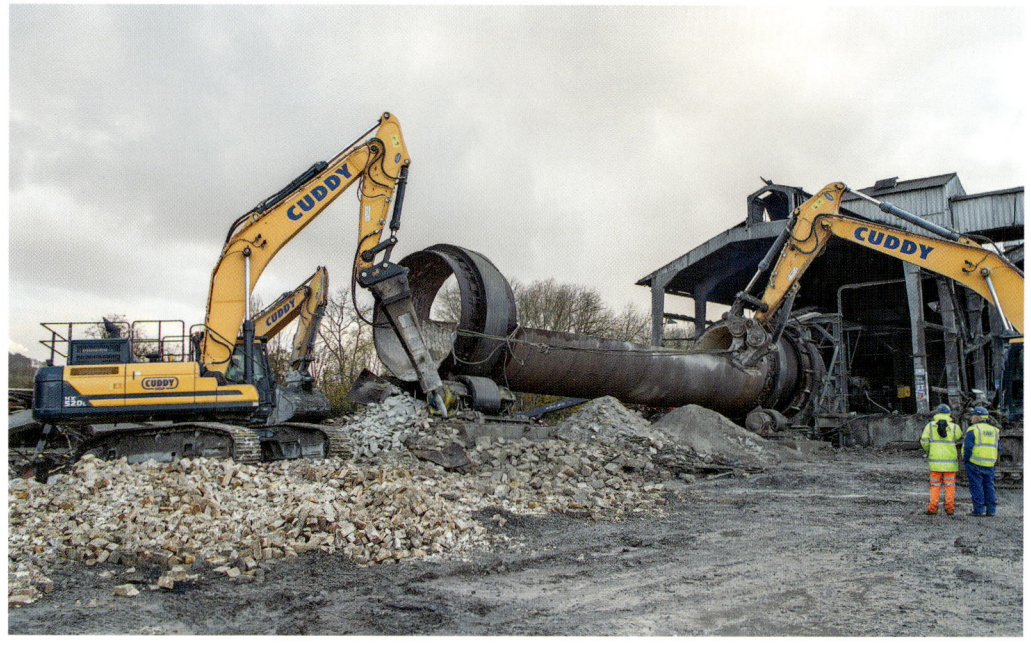

It would take all three excavators to pull and push this very last section of kiln off of its support rollers. 17 November 2016.

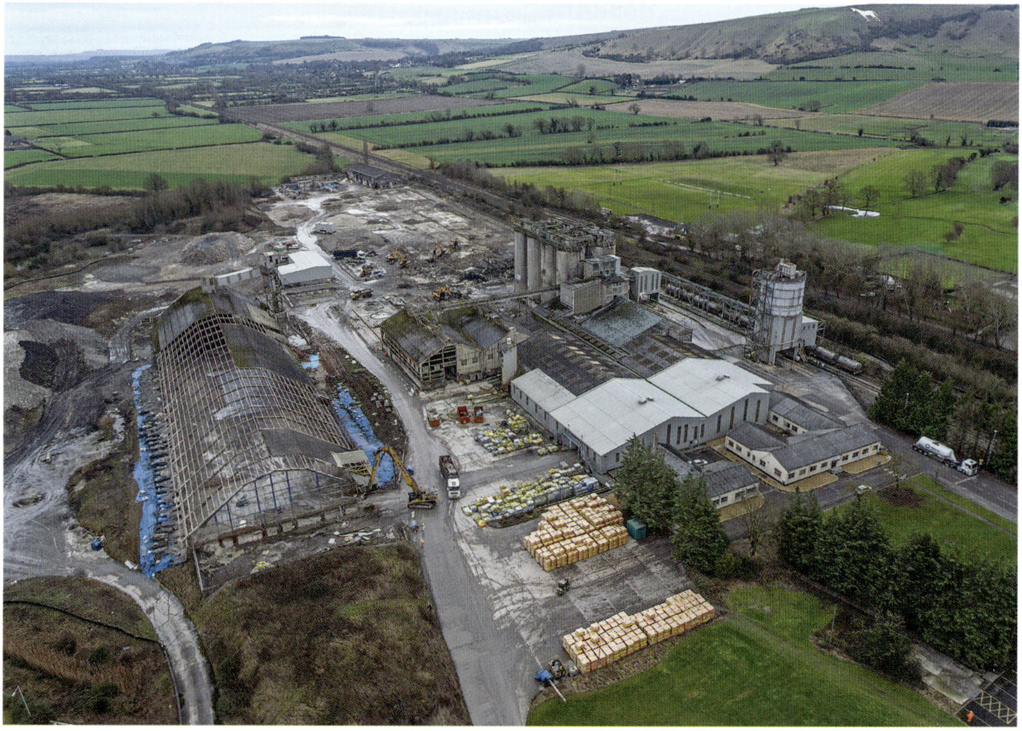

Demolition of the clinker shed is underway. 10 January 2017.

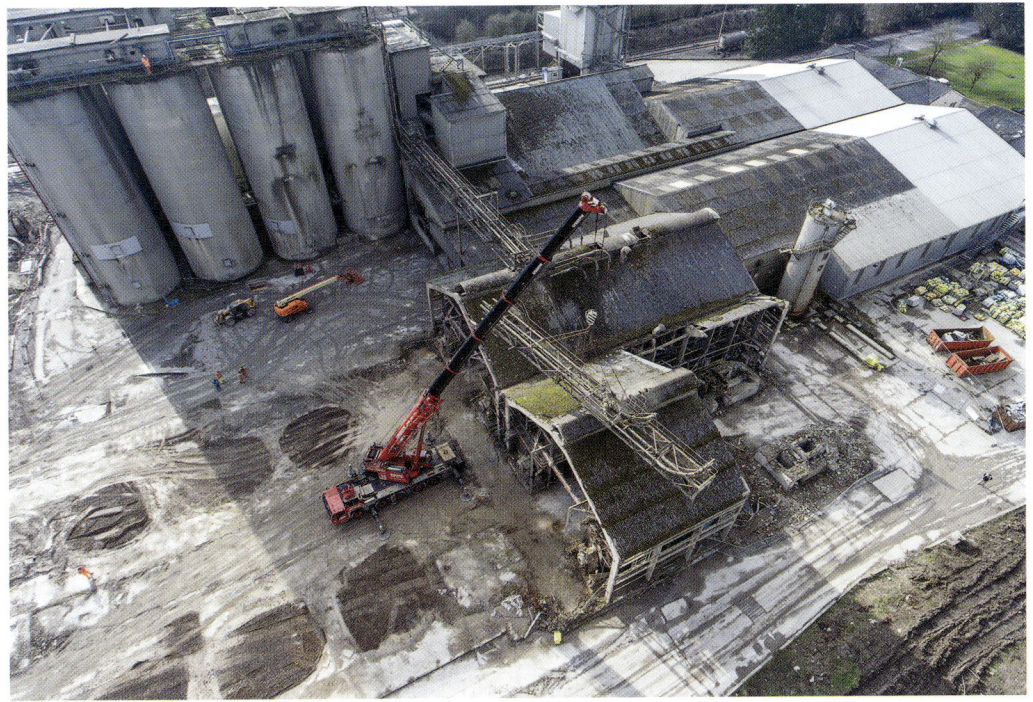

The silo pipe bridge being dismantled. 18 February 2017.

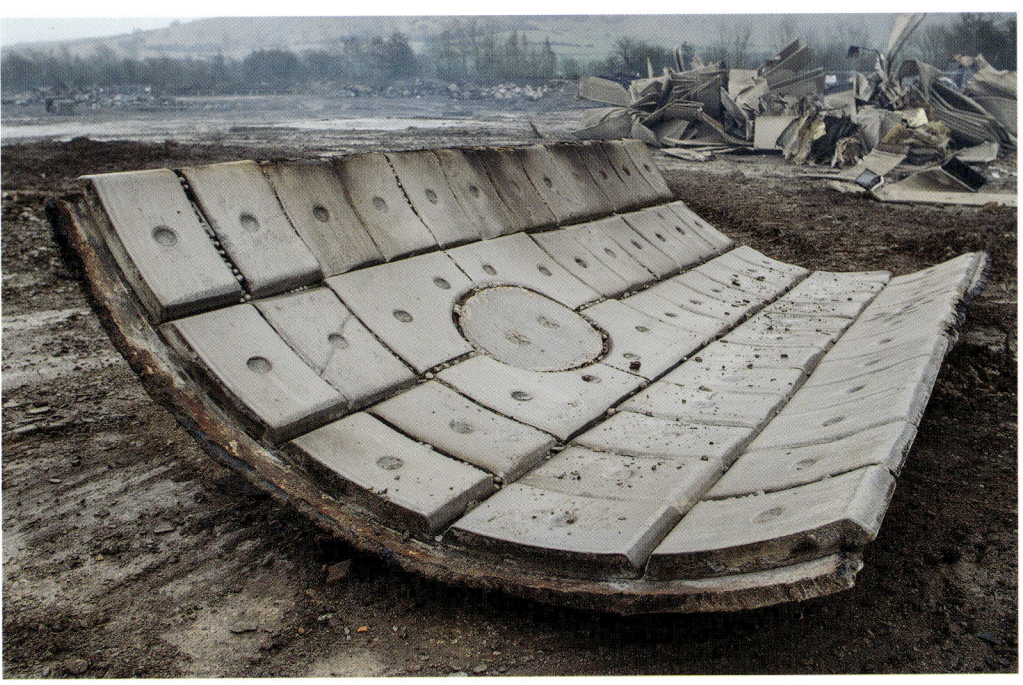

A section from one of the four grinding mills. The steel liners had an eighteen-month lifespan. 22 February 2017.

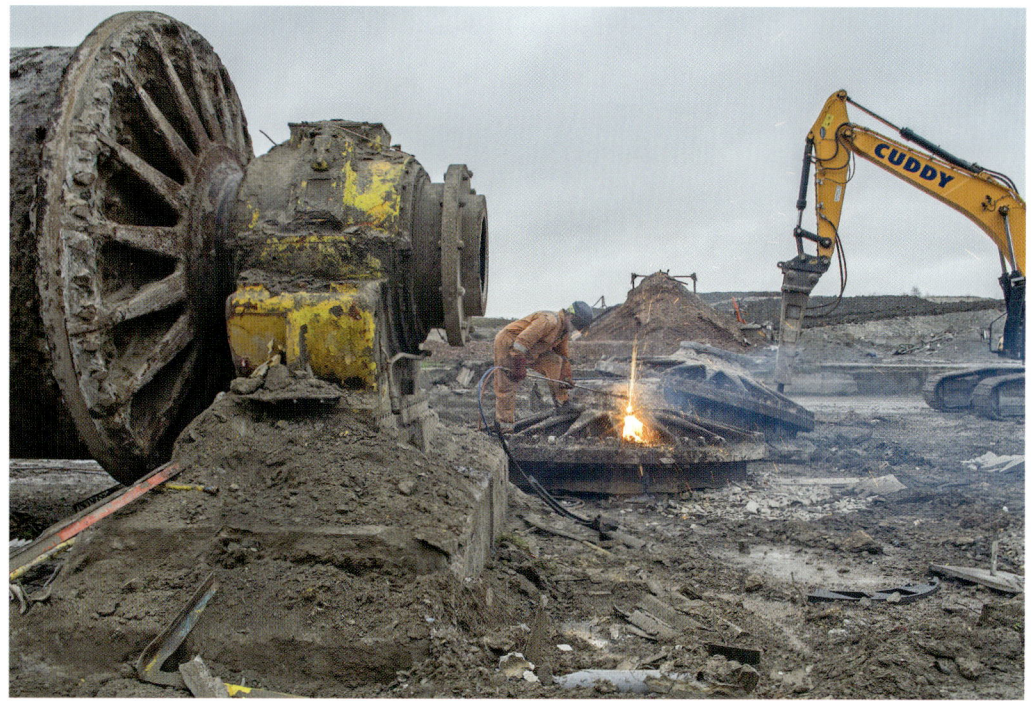

The grinding mill end walls being cut into smaller, more manageable pieces. 22 February 2017.

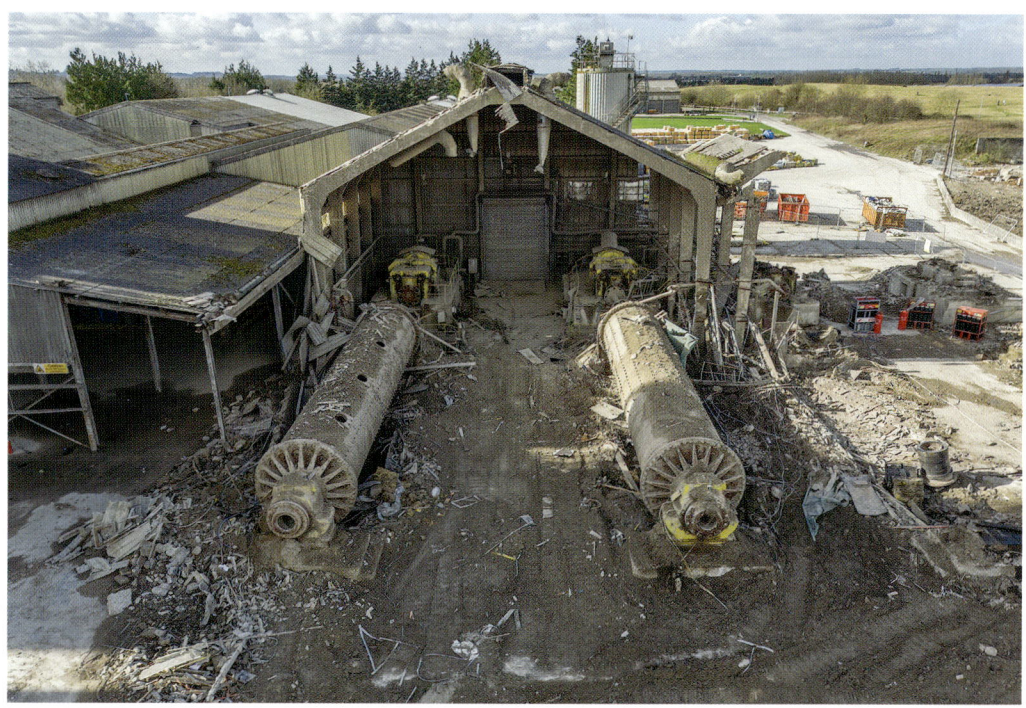

The last two grinding mills waiting to be demolished. 26 February 2017.

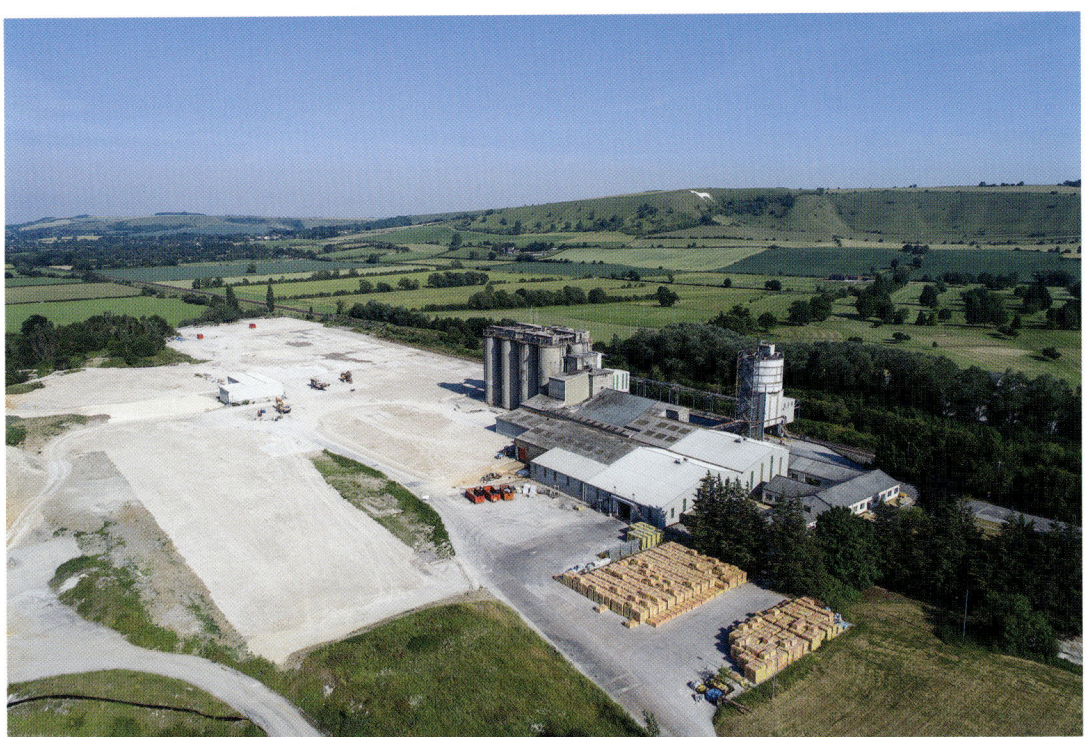

The demolished site.

Chapter 10

The End of Cement Production at Westbury

The second to last picture in this book, taken on 30 January 2009, marks the end of a forty-seven-year chapter in the history of Westbury Cement Works. Unfortunately it was a history that didn't last quite as long as Mr Reiss had predicted during the opening ceremony back in 1963. The employees gathered on the lawn outside the offices for one last group photograph, and it would be the last shift for many in this picture when the first round of redundancies was made. A second round of redundancies were made in

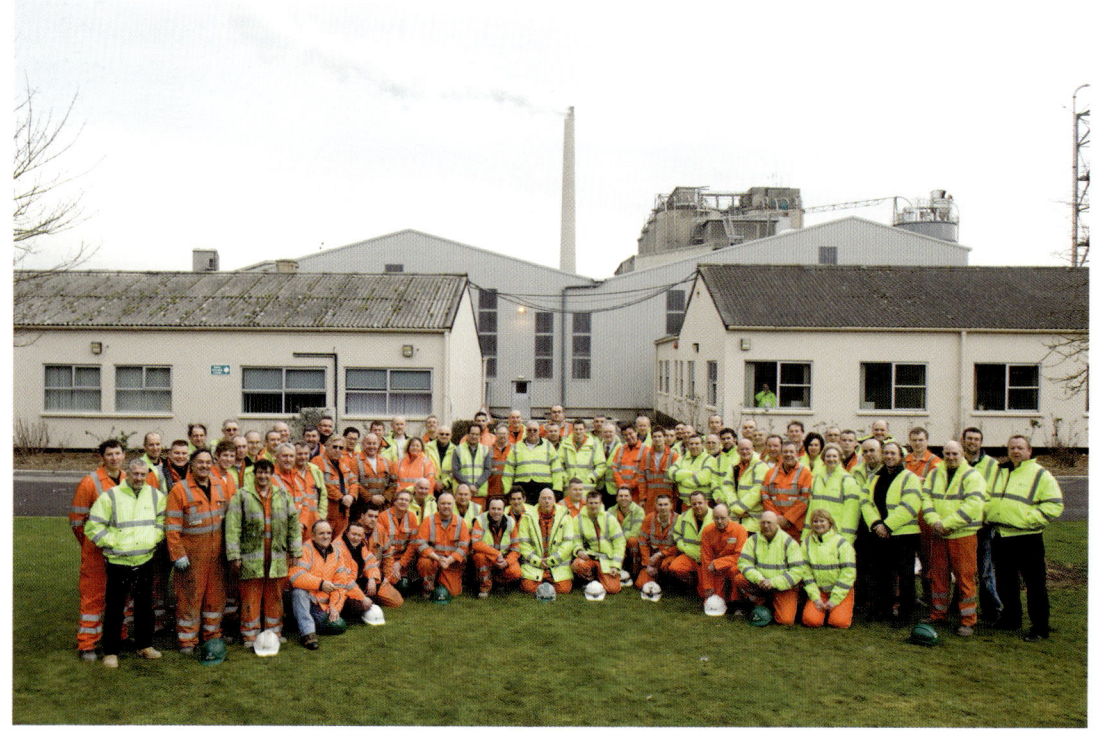

April 2009, when Kiln No. 2 was finally mothballed. Today, the works is still in use, but only as a distribution depot, and only fifteen employees remain.

As I know is also the case for the works employees, both past and present, Westbury Cement Works will always hold a place in my heart. It showed me that a place of work can mean a huge amount to its employees. It showed me how strong a workplace community can be. It showed me that even though some people complained about it and thought it was an eyesore, there was also a hidden, beautiful side to it, with the wildlife that lived on and around the site.

Now the works moves into a new chapter of its life. As I write this in May 2018, planning permission is being sought for the development of a rail-served slab track manufacturing facility. If the planning permission is successful it will ultimately bring employment to the local area and, given that some of the infrastructure is already there, will have minimal impact on the area. It may even create a workplace that means as much to its employees as this farewell message that was written on the wall of the control room shows.

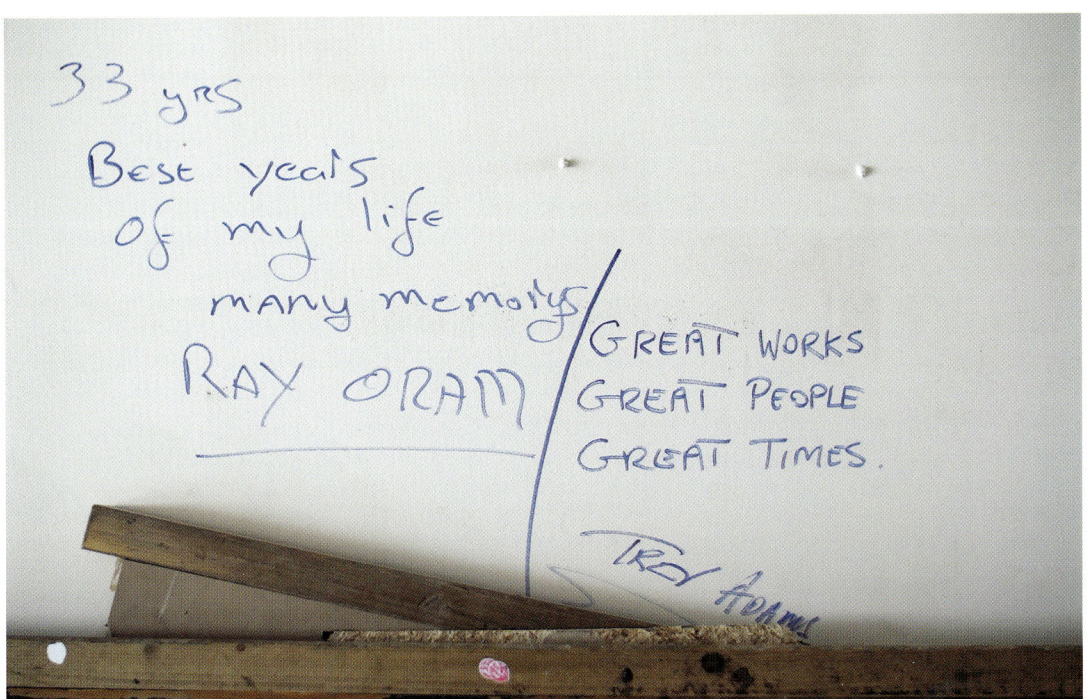

Acknowledgements

All black and white pictures and employee pictures courtesy Tarmac Ltd.

I would like to express my most sincere thanks to the following:

First of all, to all at Amberley Publishing. Thank you for going with the idea for this book. It means a great deal to me and I know that it means a lot to the employees both past and present at the works.

To Andy Burden and Rob Smith, for the initial idea about the works. To Andy again, for spending hours at the works helping me film and photograph the demolition.

At the works, I don't think that I could ever thank Nigel Osman (now site manager) enough: these pages wouldn't exist without your help. Thank you for putting up with me on my many site visits, for your photography, for answering my many, many questions and thank you for introducing me to something that I never knew existed – the site's wonderful wildlife.

To Tarmac, for allowing me on site and for allowing this book to happen and to all the Tarmac staff that I met – thank you for being friendly and helpful. Also, for supplying the old Blue Circle material that was used for reference and technical and historical accuracy.

To Cuddy Group, for letting me film and photograph them working on the demolition. Your crew were so friendly and accommodating, it made covering the demolition so much easier.

To Peter Pugh, for his superb book *The History of the Blue Circle* – an invaluable source as I put this book together.

At Bristol City Museum & Art Gallery I would like to thank Deborah Hutchinson for access to the museum and for ensuring that I was scientifically accurate with 'Deadly Doris'. Your passion and enthusiasm for your work is truly commendable.

To Simon Carpenter, for providing me with the discovery story of 'Deadly Doris'.

To Peter Milner, for your piloting skills when I needed two drones in action.

To Louis Smith, for your graphics skills and help at the works – sorry for that early start!

To Roger Martindale, for your help with the amazing peregrines and all things wildlife-related.

And to the Heritage Center at Westbury, for allowing me access to the material relating to the works. Places like this are important to ensure that local communities, histories and lives are not forgotten.

For their memories and stories of life at the works I would also like to give a special thanks to Chris Easton, who was employed at the works from 1967 to 2009 but is sadly no longer with us, to Clive Shelbourne, who was an employee from 1968 to 2003, and to Ken Ireland, who was employed at the works from 1963 to 1977.